DEADLINES AND OVERTIMES

Collected Writings on Sports and Life

BILL LYON

A *Philadelphia Inquirer* Book

D1416809

Camino Books, Inc.
Philadelphia

Manufactured in the United States of America

1 2 3 4 5   12 11 10 09

Library of Congress Cataloging–in–Publication Data

Lyon, Bill, 1938–
  Deadlines and overtimes: collected writings on sports and life / Bill Lyon
    p. cm.
  ISBN 978–1–933822–16–7 (alk. paper)
  1. Sports—Pennsylvania—Philadelphia—History. 2. Sports—History.
3. Professional sports—Pennsylvania—Philadelphia—History. 4. Sports
journalism—United States—History. 5. Philadelphia inquirer. I. Philadelphia
inquirer. II. Title.

  GV584.5.P46L96 2009
  796.09748'11—dc22   2009017686

Cover and interior design: Jerilyn Bockorick

This book is available at a special discount on bulk purchases for promotional,
business, and educational use.

Publisher
Camino Books, Inc.
P.O. Box 59026
Philadelphia, PA 19102

www.caminobooks.com

Contents

Family is all.

Ours has wept and laughed, mourned and celebrated,
sometimes at the same time, and sustained each other
in times of turmoil and tumult, doubt and certitude.
To them, my gratitude, and to them, this dedication:

To my wife, Ethel. None are braver.

To our sons, John and Jim. They make a parent proud.

To our daughter-in-law, Sandy. Angel of mercy.

To my mother, Harriet, who first said to me:
"Maybe you should try writing."

To our grandsons, Evan and Joshua, who remind me
that the Circle of Life is a precious thing indeed.

And to you, loyal readers, who have always
felt like an extended family.

One more time: Group hug.

Introduction

In the spring of 1956, the man who would hire me said, Yes, that is correct. If you can string together some reasonably coherent sentences, we shall publish them. And pay you.

My adolescent mind reeled at the thought: Money for writing. Surely, I have died and gone to heaven.

Not wanting to dampen my enthusiasm, the man thoughtfully refrained from mentioning that even before it would have a chance to yellow and fade, the deathless prose I would be offering up would serve as a repository for eggshells and coffee grounds, as lining for the bottoms of bird cages, and as bladder training for puppies who were equally enthusiastic.

Now then, about the money...

Uh, well, that will come, after deductions, to 84 dollars and 56 cents. For two weeks. Payday is every other Wednesday. Truth is, I'd have done it for nothing. That's how deeply words had gotten their hooks in me.

Report for work at eight a.m., the man said. I was there at six. Wired.

He gave me one set of instructions: The overriding mission of this profession is to comfort the afflicted...and afflict the comfortable. Lofty goals, indeed, but difficult to determine exactly how that was applicable when I spent the first summer taking Little League box scores, interviewing the canned preserves winners at country fairs, and writing obituaries.

Patience, the man had said. Your time shall come. But first an apprenticeship must be served.

I yearned to chronicle tales of heroic men and women at play. The man nodded. He understood. We turn to the front page to read of man's failures and shortcomings; we turn to the sports pages to read of his triumphs. Reality in one place, refuge in the other.

The first athlete to affect me viscerally was a football player. Butkus. Dick Butkus. I saw him in high school, then college (Illinois), and finally with the Chicago Bears. Under *middle linebacker*, they should run his picture. There was a primitive quality about him that was riveting. His hands were gnarled and misshapen, and he was bowlegged, like a croquet wicket in cleats. When he crouched behind the line of scrimmage, the breath coming like steam from his mouth, all you could think was, "Blood on the moon."

A running back who had been caught in one of those violent embraces still had vacant eyes and spaghetti legs after the game was over. Butkus had met him head on, like he was a long–lost friend.

"Wasn't the fullback supposed to lead you into the hole on that play?"

"Uh–huh," he mumbled. So where was he?

"Dunno. Think maybe Butkus ate him."

Of all the athletes I have seen, one rises above them: Ali.

He was liquid grace. In a barbaric sport, he was so supple and skilled that you forgot he was making the other man in the ring bleed. But more than anything, he could improvise in the midst of chaos. Here was a man who really could dance between the raindrops.

And he was marvelously verbal and mentally agile, able to captivate whole rooms of people who came intending to harpoon him and left, instead, singing his praises.

This may or may not be true, but if it isn't, it should be: The only time he was left without a comeback was when a stewardess stopped to say: "Buckle your seat belt, Mister Ali."

"Superman don't need no seat belt," he said, eyes twinkling.

And without missing a beat, the stewardess said sweetly: "Superman don't need no plane, either."

I toiled in the vineyards in the Midwest—three papers in 16 years in Illinois and Indiana, and then, in the summer of '72 was lured to Philadelphia.

"The Big Time," I crowed to the family.

"You're gonna love it. Great sports city. Just great. Winners everywhere."

So we arrived in this promised Big Time just in time to see Steve Carlton win 27 games and the rest of the Phillies combined only 32. The Eagles would conclude another season of spectacular failure, going 2–11–1. The Flyers would be eliminated from the playoffs on the very last game of the regular season. And the 76ers established a record for futility and ineptitude that remains to this day: nine wins and 73 defeats.

Good God, I thought, what have I gotten us into?

But it got better. Really it did.

There was a time in the misty long ago when all our teams were winners, and with monotonous regularity. Ah, those were the days, my friend; we thought they'd never end…

The Renaissance began in the spring of 1974. The Flyers won the first of consecutive Stanley Cups, and even though hockey was fairly new to the city, the fans, starved for a champion, mobilized by the millions and turned out for a parade that was larger than even that for the end of World War II.

License plates proliferated with the slogan: "Only the Lord Saves More Than Bernie." Bernard Marcel Parent, a French Canadian, became an honorary Philadelphian—for life. For two magical, mystical seasons, he was an impregnable fortress in goal. The leader was a fang–toothed, cheap–shotting, diabetic instigator and igniter named Bobby Clarke…of the Flin Flon Clarkes. The team's good luck charm was Kate Smith, whose rendition of "God Bless America" is still trotted out for big games. And the coach, the enigmatic Fred Shero, wrote on the locker room blackboard the day his team would win their first Cup words that raise hackles even now: "Win Today and We Walk Together Forever." Many of those Flyers live in the area to this day…and they still don't have to buy a round.

The 76ers began the 1972–73 season with 17 straight losses and didn't improve appreciably on that dismal start. Shortly after that debacle, they began to build: Doug Collins, Andrew (The Boston Strangler) Toney, Joe (Jelly Bean) Bryant, Lloyd (World B) Free, Bobby (The White Shadow) Jones and, of course, a certain Doctor. The coach was Billy Cunningham, alias The Kangaroo Kid; he would leap from the bench to protest a call with such fury that he would split the seat out of his trousers.

One day, the general manager, Pat Williams, came to the owner, Fitz Dixon, and let slip this exciting prospect: "We have a chance to acquire"…dramatic pause here… "Julius Erving." To which Dixon replied: "Fine and dandy, Pat. Now tell me, who is Julius Erving?"

"Uh, well," Williams stammered, "he's sort of the Babe Ruth of basketball."

The good Doctor J was acquired for six million dollars, probably the best money the franchise ever spent.

Which brings us to your—all together now—E-A-G-L-E-S. Chronic losers they were, and yet the Bumbling Birds' season ticket base never wavered, even with 11 losing seasons in a row. Eagles fans, it was often said, could teach loyalty to a dog.

The turnaround started with the hiring of a head coach who not only had no pro experience, but came from the other side of the continent…California, for God's sake. No pretty Surfer Boy is going to last a Philadelphia minute here in the grit and grime of the Northeast. And yet Dick Vermeil would end up owning the city, his face on Blue Cross billboards years after he left.

You always start with a quarterback, and Vermeil brought in the self–anointed Polish rifle, or more familiarly, Jaws. As the boos rained down on the quarterback's helmeted head during a dreary early performance, Vermeil told Ron Jaworski: "These people have been changing quarterbacks for years. But no more. You're my QB and I'm sticking with you." And so he did…all the way to the Super Bowl.

And now we come to the Fightin's.

No professional sports franchise has lost more games than the Phillies. And few have as forlorn an unraveling as the Great Collapse of 1964. But for a decade or so, from the mid–1970s to the mid–'80s, they won and won and won, although one of their managers, Danny Ozark, couldn't quite grasp the immutable, mathematical certainty that being four games out of first with three to play meant that you were eliminated. Honest.

Some wonderful performers danced across that stage: Steve Carlton and that unhittable slider that danced like a Frisbee in a high wind; Mike Schmidt, who played with a cheetah's grace and had that marvelously compact stroke; Garry Lee (three–fourths of the earth is covered by water, the rest by him) Maddox; Frank Edwin McGraw, alias Tug, the Irish leprechaun out of the bullpen, who named his pitches (the Peggy Lee fastball—Is that all there is?); and at shortstop a Tabasco sauce and red hot pepper named Larry Bowa.

In 1980, they won it all. That comes out to once every 125 years, give or take. And outsiders wonder why we're so impatient.

The year 1980 will forever be recalled as the year the vinegar changed to champagne. Each of Philadelphia's four major sports teams played for the world championship. Yes, only the Fightin's prevailed, but for one enchanted year, we were awash in an embarrassment of riches.

Three years later, we would get another parade. Do you remember this: "Fo…Fo…Fo"? Moses Malone's bodacious guarantee. He missed by only one that prediction of a playoff sweep. The parade began at City Hall and ended in center field of the late and mostly unlamented Veterans Stadium.

From time to time, I was offered employment in other precincts. I never considered moving. I came here a Pilgrim, a naïve Heartlander, and I fell in love with this city, this vibrant city, this city that boils with such sporting passion, that has a matchless capacity for suffering and for persisting, a city whose teams can send it soaring into paroxysms of joy or plunging into black holes of despair. Occasionally at the same time.

This is the city with such a rich and varied past, the city where Wilt dunked and Concrete Charlie tackled. Where the Doctor skywalked and Moving Van ran. Where Schmitty homered and Smokin' Joe knocked people into next week.

And this is the city that is home to legendary venues. The Palestra, that great gray cathedral that on basketball nights becomes such a charming little passion pit. And hoary, venerable Franklin Field, where last the Iggles won a championship. And Boathouse Row, where the night lights glisten and where, in spring chill and summer heat, the waters roil under the piston strokes of the oars.

Leave? Not hardly. Where else do they suffer more grandly or demonstrate such abiding resiliency?

There is a popular theory that the city is jinxed, the fans too demanding, the negativity draped like a black shroud over Billy Penn's hat. It is tempting to succumb to the notion of some giant hex. I do not. Sports, like life, goes in cycles. One day, the pendulum will swing the other way.

One day. Someday. "Just you wait and see" day.

The bane of our profession is contained in one word: Deadline.

It will give you the screaming sweats. Sometimes it will give you 37 seconds to write 500 words. Yes, that is an exaggeration, but only a slight one.

There is nothing quite so daunting and yet, in a perverse way, so exhilarating, as racing to beat a deadline. It will leave you, to quote the cowboy, feeling like you've been rode hard and put up wet.

When I first asked an editor man what happens when you miss your deadline, he looked at me and shook his head sadly, sighed heavily, and said very slowly: "You do not understand. You do not miss a deadline. Ever. There is no excuse. Not even death. That's why it's called a DEADline."

To that end, I want to introduce you to the late Harry Hoffman, who was a sportswriter for an Atlantic City newspaper some years back. Harry was covering a Phillies opening–day game at Connie Mack Stadium. The home team had lost, as was more common than not in those days, and Harry ran from the press box down to the clubhouse, procured some quotes, ran back to the press box, typed his story, then ran to the nearest telephone booth to dictate his story.

He was into the third paragraph when he felt something prodding him in the back, and a low, gravelly voice said: "This is a holdup. Gimme all you got."

Harry obliged…and kept right on dictating all the while.

He fished out his wallet. Two sentences. His watch. Three sentences. Finally, in exasperation, Harry snapped: "Hurry it up, will you, pal? I'm on deadline here."

Harry, old friend, this one's for you.

A final thought. About sports.

Do they have value beyond simple entertainment? I think so. Even with all the arrogance and avarice, the coddled mercenaries, the Machiavellian agents, the loutish and drunken behavior in the stands, even with all that, sport is still filled, almost always, with redemption and atonement.

Sport is where, for all that is petty and pig–headed here on the third rock from the sun, we are privileged to witness pride and passion, valor and resiliency, perseverance and persistence...great, shining examples of the fierce, unbending indomitability of the human spirit.

It gives us that rarest of gifts.

Hope.

1

To Philadelphia . . . with Love

Ice Skating in Hades

OCTOBER 30, 2008

And so at 9:58 in the East, on a cold and brittle autumn night, Brad Lidge, the perfect pitcher in an imperfect game, threw strike three past a Tampa Bay pinch hitter, and the baseball team that has always been one tantalizing pitch away from heartbreak won the 2008 World Series.

Lidge, the cold-eyed closer, nailed down his 48th save in 48 opportunities, leaped part way to the moon, then sank to his knees and motioned for catcher Carlos Ruiz to hurry to him. Ryan Howard fell on top of both of them, setting off seismographs in four states.

And thus endeth one of the most bizarre and controversial games ever played in the World Series, complete with a 46-hour wait between innings, and how fitting that was, for this is Philadelphia, after all: cradle of liberty, acid reflux, angst, anxiety, and the sure and certain belief that we are doomed forever to walk along the Boulevard of Busted Dreams.

But not now. Not this time. No, you can go ice skating in Hades now. The Phillies have broken the "Hundred Season Drought." The franchise of 10,000 losses is a winner.

The air already smells cleaner. The women are beautiful. Food tastes better. The shroud of dread has been pulled away.

This is a team that took its cue from a good ol' country boy, a baseball lifer with an abiding attachment to, and respect for, the game. Charlie Manuel has spent four years as manager of the Phillies. They call that doing hard time.

He endured cruel slander without complaint. He is a man with rhino hide and the courage of his convictions, a man whose loyalty to his players has been unshakable. There was, he was certain, a title awaiting him.

He was rocked during the postseason by the death of his mother, and last night, asked what she would be doing about now, he replied: "Laughing and giggling and hollering and telling us, and everyone, how good a team I had."

As soon as Lidge delivered the final pitch, an unhittable slider, Manuel and his coaches embraced in the dugout. They are old, battle-worn warriors, each with the scars that they wear like badges of honor.

"I can take the criticism," Manuel said. "I'm old enough and experienced enough. You know what, until you win something a lot of times, you're going to be criticized. Yeah, sometimes it's hard to take some personal criticism, but at the same time that's part of being mentally tough, and also it's part of being professional."

Charlie Manuel is more man than the howler monkeys who vilified him.

"The things that go on here," he said of the World Series, "it kind of gets hectic and you definitely can lose focus. And if you're not careful, you've got to keep things in perspective. To win is hard. To win a World Series is probably harder."

The Phillies have been committing baseball for 126 years and this is their second championship. Their history is a tortured one.

But Lidge offered exactly the right perspective when he said: "This is our time right now, and I don't give a crap about all the rest."

Yes, the time for haunting is past. What has gone before now shrinks in importance. The vinegar turns to champagne.

Asked if he and the rest of the Phillies fully grasped the magnitude of what they had done for the city, Cole Hamels, the pitching prodigy who was MVP of the World Series, said: "When we come back, when we're all old and retired and we come back and they still stand up, giving us a standing ovation like they do to the guys of the 1980 World Series. The fans added to our confidence. These fans, they could taste it as much as we could."

Well, maybe not that much. It's been 25 years since the last championship, and Hamels, who is 24, was not yet born when the 76ers won it all.

But the core of this team is young and brims with exuberance. Surely more titles will come. We are, after all, due. All this persistent enduring in the face of so much torment surely must carry a reward.

The last word, fittingly, goes to Charlie Manuel: "When I saw that last out, I kind of looked up and watched the fans and our players and I knew it was over. And I said, you know what, we just won the World Series. Like, we're champions. Actually, it was bigger than I actually felt like it was."

Just wait until the parade.

With This World Series Ring, I...

It is a fragile, tenuous relationship, this marriage of professional athletes and a defiantly prideful city.

As with most marriages, there is, from time to tempestuous time, broken crockery scattered on the floor, passion wasted on things not worth the price, hurtful words that cannot be recalled, and on bittersweet occasions, a tearful make-up.

Which brings us to Philadelphia and its baseball team, wed for better or for worse for 126 years now, which is a remarkable, even miraculous, tenure when you think on it.

The city's hard-edged reputation precedes itself, and athletes are wary. Like wolves that smell roasting meat, they circle warily around the campfire, slinking uncertainly about in the shadows, wondering, fretting: "Do I really want to play here, in front of these lynch mobs?"

But every great once in a while, each side is brought to realize the true depth of its marriage. Like, for example, when you win a World Series.

Secretly, we glory in our hard-edged reputation. We take a perverse pride in being known as the proving ground of sports—relentlessly demanding, quick to judge, quicker still to root out the slackers and the charlatans.

But beneath that rhino hide of ours lies a marshmallow: gooey, soft, yielding. You bust a gut trying, you spend your blood and assorted body parts for us, and we will melt.

But even we surprise ourselves when the chance comes along. Like, say, a parade of champions. World Series champions. Or, to use the earthy Anglo–Saxon term for fornication as memorably uttered by Chase Utley: World F——— Champions.

To a man, the Phillies were overwhelmed by the parade and the reception. They were engulfed by a sea of people. They thought they knew what they would see, but it was so much more sweeping than that.

And they were made to grasp the magnitude of this marriage, made to understand the umbilical that binds city and team with an almost mystical force.

"This is way better than I ever expected," said manager Charlie Manuel.

They chant his name now, shout it from the rooftops. Four years ago, he was derided as a clueless country bumpkin. Now, and forever, he will occupy a place in the Hall of Winners. Such is the power of a championship.

But why? What is the appeal of a band of mercenaries with bat, ball and glove winning a tournament?

It is a civic validation of sorts. We didn't actually win anything ourselves, but our team did, and by extension we did, too. We're not suddenly smarter. Or better looking. But it feels like it, feels like there's pride back in our stride.

And there is the matter of welcome distraction, an escape from all that besets us. That's the gift players bestow on the city. And the city, in turn, showers them with…well, you've seen the parade pictures.

The players, caught by surprise at the outpouring of affection, try to return it in kind. They pledge their own fealty. They will be a Phillie, and a Philadelphian, till the day they die, promise.

Cole Hamels, who has a perspective to match that killer dead-fish change-up, talked about coming back, old and retired and maybe a little fat, and being accorded the standing ovation and the devotion still showered on the 1980 champions.

Unlike many things in life, this is forever. Or until the next parade. Which could be as soon as next year.

The core of this team is, after all, young. There is every reason to think its best ball is still ahead of it.

Hamels said he couldn't wait to float down Broad Street again.

And again. And again.

For a time, at least, the negativity withers like things dying on the November vines. The marriage between wary player and defiantly prideful city flourishes.

A new dawn? Consider this sign along the parade route: "I Promise Never To Boo Again."

Here, that is the highest compliment.

A Fine Madness

NOVEMBER 1, 2008

It was one of those pristine, crystalline, sun-splashed, green-and-gold, shadow-streaked days that October, the best month of the year, favors us with from time to time: a day perfect for, say, a parade.

By happy circumstance, we just happened to have one scheduled. And, oh, was it glorious. Well worth the wait, and no matter that the wait had felt like forever and a day.

The Phillies, you might have heard, won the World Series the other day.

The city, of course, was the very model of decorum and restraint. Or, in the words of Ryan Howard, the Big Bopper: "This is the craziest place on earth."

Yes. And damn proud of it, too.

A delightful delirium gripped Philadelphia yesterday. Broad Street was transformed into a Canyon of Heroes. Fathers and mothers brought sons and daughters because, well because it represents the symbolic closing of a circle, because one day of truancy can be educational in its own way. And, oh by the way, there is, *too,* crying in baseball.

Blizzards of confetti swirled. There were horses and bicycles and foot police, flat beds and floats and double deckers. And a tsunami-sized wake clogging the streets as the parade crawled past.

The parade…and oh by the way again, it's OK to say the P-word now. The curse is no more.

And oh by the way one last time, the editor man is poking me in the ribs with that pointy stick again and asking, so how does this parade rank with the others?

"The others" is not a category requiring exhaustive research, there having been only three others in the last 34 years. Memory is elusive and from time to time you cannot recall what you had for lunch, let alone a previous century. Nonetheless, I shall make a determined stab at it.

On a splendid, sunny day in the spring of 1974, I took a fourth–floor, open–window perch to watch the Flyers parade a certain vessel of some repute. Hockey was new to Philadelphia, but Lord Stanley's Cup acquired instant popularity. At that point, the city was every bit as victory–starved as they were until this past Wednesday.

It is probably not an exaggeration to suggest that fully half of those who came to the parade had never been within shouting distance of a puck. The parade was an excuse to party, which they did with impressive and relentless determination.

Police guessed the crowd to be in excess of two million. Many of them, enjoying this fine May day, sat on ledges. Fortunately, none toppled over. Veterans said the assembly rivaled the end of World War II, historic indeed.

There was one serious miscalculation. The players themselves were loaded into convertibles. With the tops down. Which allowed cans of beer to be passed from the festive crowd directly into the Flyers' thirsty maws. The parade crawled along, barely a block an hour, and by its end, well, to this day when you say to some of the players, "Some parade, eh?" they reply: "I'll take your word for it."

The Phillies, 1980. Police guessed that parade drew close to a million. I decided to walk it. Bad mistake.

The late and dearly missed Frank Edwin McGraw, a.k.a. Tug, has become the enduring image of those festivities through three photographs.

The first is that arms–up, leaping Irish two step he danced in joy after firing the last pitch.

The second is Tug brandishing the *Daily News* with its screaming headline: "WE WIN."

The third is "The Three Amigos," viewed from left to right: Tug, Pete Rose and Larry Bowa. They celebrated as robustly as they played.

They rode on flatbeds, and every other block or so, inebriated fans would attempt to leap on and join The Three Amigos. But the police had four–legged deterrents.

"I got a whole new level of respect and appreciation for horses that day," Tug said later.

The 76ers, 1983. A bright, exquisite June day. The crowd estimate was 1.7 million. They had a flatbed for the media. Miles better than trying to walk it.

One of the flatbeds blew a tire just as the parade started. Somehow, even though listing to one side and wobbling drunkenly, it made it all the way to the finish. Was that quintessential Philadelphia, or what? Go the distance no matter what.

Those were the Sixers of Doc and Moses, Mo and Andrew, Bobby and Billy C. The parade ended just beyond second base, Julius Erving and Billy Cunningham lifting the trophy that glinted in the sun like spun gold.

The Phillies, 2008. Tried watching it on TV: much preferable to trying to wade through pedestrian gridlock. My bladder also applauded the decision.

And how did we do the fourth time around? We are a quick study, and seem to have gotten the hang of it.

It would be a nice habit to acquire.

Faithful To a Fault

This is for you.

You who have endured defeat after numbing defeat and never defected, who stayed on even when there was no good reason for doing so.

This is for you and your patient-beyond-all-understanding ancestors, who have remained truer-than-the-bluest-sky true . . . to the very end . . . and beyond.

You and the generations that came before you, redefining what loyalty means, handing over your hearts and your money even while knowing the first will get broken and the second comes without a refund.

This is for all of you, for the more than 120 million of you, who have slogged resolutely along this trail of tears, who have sworn passionate pledges of allegiance and bought tickets to see the major-league franchise of Philadelphia attempt to commit baseball for the last century and a quarter.

More than 120 million of you paying your way in, keeping the turnstiles clicking merrily. And that is the number that matters. That is the number that is, in its own way, far more meaningful than 10,000 defeats.

That is the number that we should be celebrating in the midst of the 10 Grand Mourning.

Because that is the number that speaks to the heart of the Phillies fan—a curious, ambivalent mixture of idealism and fatalism, at once demanding and yet forgiving, and above all, resilient, durable, refusing to yield, for whom surrender is unthinkable. Has there ever lived a creature to rival the Phillies fan? Harder to discourage than a sidewalk weed. Always coming back for more. Go ahead, load up and take another shot. We endure, we persevere, we do not discourage.

The passion runs bone–deep, sometimes so deep that it pushes a fan over the edge. A few years ago, a distressed Phillies fan and hacker broke into the computers of some Philadelphia writers and began to flood the country with messages of vitriol about the people who run his beloved baseball team.

I was one of the hacker's victims. For days his e-mails flowed in unstoppable torrents from my laptop to people I had never met, and vice versa. The messages were always an assault on Phillies management and frequently were laced with profanity.

They went to complete strangers, who replied to me with puzzlement ("Who are you and why are you doing this?") and with litigious threats

("You'll be hearing from my attorney") and with dark rage ("I know a man named Guido who can make you walk funny").

The hacker eventually was caught by the FBI, stood trial, and was convicted of 79 charges.

I now admit, from the comfort of time elapsed, to a slight stab of sympathy. All the misguided soul wanted, as his attorney argued, was the widest possible audience for his screeds of frustration against Phillies management. He was, to borrow from the movie *Network,* mad as hell and he wasn't going to take it anymore. It may have been the only time in history when a man went to jail because he loved his baseball team way, way too much.

Ten thousand of anything qualifies as a group effort. So Phillies fans love wisely, if not well, and it may be argued that, in an ironic and perverse way, their eternal devotion works against the improvement of their team.

Boycott the Fightin's, goes a popular refrain, and force management to spend. Hit 'em where they'll feel it most, at the turnstile.

Ultimately, though, these calls for revolt fall on deaf ears, because true fans of the Fightin's simply cannot exorcise whatever it is that possesses them. For better or worse . . . in sickness and in another season of gut-shot agony and fading finish . . . they are wedded and they will not be put asunder.

Besides, there is an irresistible pull. We are tied to the game by a common umbilical, a rite of passage that is handed down. It goes from "Wanna have a catch?" to "Wanna go to a game?"

Remember your first time? Has the grass ever been as impossibly green?

So then, 10,000 is about to be reached. It will be a while, 1200 of them or so, before they approach 10,000 wins. Until then, they will continue to be rooted along by those who, disgruntled after another galling loss, swear they are through. Never watch them again. Never. Never. Never.

And, of course, that vow will melt silently away. The Fightin's are our guilty pleasure.

On celebrate 10000.com, one of the websites that has chronicled the trail of tears, a fan wrote of a grandfather, a Mr. Julian Thomas, who, upon reaching his 100th birthday, was asked the obligatory question. And his reply to the secret of his longevity was this: "Waiting for the Phillies to win another World Series."

Mr. Thomas, this one is for you.

Spectrum: Thunderdome

JULY 16, 2008

At its ear-shattering best, the Spectrum was Thunderdome, a Niagara of noise, waves of shuddering sound roiling to the rafters, the echoes ricocheting off the walls.

When a Philadelphia team was playing, you could stand out in the parking lot and the crowd noise would tell you how the home team was faring—if they were winning, the passion was as raw and bone-deep as a January night, an unrelenting, urging surge of support.

And if they were losing . . . ah, well, then it was a mournful wail, so haunting that wolf packs a thousand miles away lifted their muzzles to the heavens and bayed at the moon in sympathetic reply.

To this day, it is claimed that way up there in the cold, cold north there are wolves that know how to boo.

For three full decades and bits and pieces of two more, the Spectrum served its purpose uncommonly well—it was more than just another antiseptic arena, it was one of our civic cathedrals, a signature profile, its lights emitting an inviting glow, tempting, bidding you.

Crooners crooned there. Dr. J dunked there. Sinatra in a tux, Doc walking on air. Smooth. Silk-on-satin smooth.

The Flyers won Stanley Cups there, won them when the sport was new here—hockey? What's hockey?—won by toothless Canadians long on grit and gristle. They came into their locker room before the deciding game to find this message written on a chalk board by their coach, the enigmatic Fred Shero: "Win today and we walk together forever."

Quite a prophecy.

Clarkie and Bernie. The Watson brothers. Moose and Hound. Big Bird and The Hammer. Lunch-pail, hard-hat athletes, hungry . . . hungry and ravenous because the big money hadn't infected their sport yet.

Even they didn't fully comprehend the impact they would have on this town. None of us could. They were the best and the brightest, and they remain so to this day.

The Blade Runners.

The Spectrum was theirs. They brawled and bashed and splattered its ice with blood—the opponents' and their own. In Philadelphia, blood plays big.

Kate Smith played big, too. In life and in records. Adopted as the Flyers' good–luck talisman, when her version of "God Bless America" was played, the Spectrum vibrated like a giant tuning fork, and the hardest of hearts suddenly found it hard to swallow.

And then the hard wood would be placed on top of the ice and the 76ers would take over. Moses and Mo. World B. Jelly Bean. The White Shadow. The Kangaroo Kid. The Boston Strangler.

Remember? They gave us a great parade: 25 years ago. Ah, boy, we know that math, don't we? All of us. Know it by heart. Know every galling, gnawing season of frustration.

Nothing lasts forever . . . well, with the exception of public television pledge drives. And now the Spectrum is coming down, the judgment, devoid of emotion, being that it has outlasted its usefulness.

So, there will soon be a tiny, precise mound of rubble and from the bones will arise new commercial ventures. The Spectrum will be the third sporting venue fatality of recent time, joining JFK Stadium and the Vet. They recede in our memory, and when summoned, now show up fuzzy and indistinct. Years hence, such a fate undoubtedly awaits the Spectrum. But its passing needs to be observed. It was home to heroes and zeros, to moments of giddy exhilaration and wrenching despair, to high drama and low comedy.

The fall of the Wachovia Spectrum thins the South Philadelphia sporting venue ranks. We are left with three playpens now, and we take them for granted. Our sports complex is a thing to be chest-thumping proud of, but of course we would prefer to find nits to pick.

I did 31 years and a small river of words in the Spectrum, hunched over at a Quasimodo trajectory in the cramped hockey press box, or wedged in along the baseline, so close to the floor I could see the whole unit—basket, backboard, stanchion, all of it—be moved by Charles Barkley at the conclusion of a two-handed breakaway dunk. No one tried to step in and take a charge against Charles.

The single best individual play I ever saw in the Spectrum was on a dank, rain-lashed night in March 1992, Duke against Kentucky in the regional finals of the NCAA tournament.

Christian Laettner took a 75-foot inbounds pass at the top of the key, faked, pivoted, and put up a jump shot that splashed the netting at the gun. As is customary in this profession, we were given 37 seconds to write 500 words.

There were a lot of deadlines in the Spectrum, a lot of nights when you looked beseechingly at all those banners draped from the rafters, pleading desperately for inspiration, asking the building to bail you out one more time.

It's only a building, the pragmatist will say, and correctly so. Concrete and steel rods. Inanimate.

Maybe so. But it is also the repository of memories, memories for which there are no replacements.

So then, let us lift a glass. And cherish the memories.

Vet I: A Grand Stage

DECEMBER 14, 2002

In some sad, perverse way, you confessed to yourself, you're going to miss that rust spot.

The one that stains the steel beam just above seat B-12 in the press box of Veterans Stadium. Home away from home for lo these many years—almost too many beyond the tallying. You and the Vet have grown old together, spending the parts of four different decades in each other's huddled company.

Over the football seasons, that rust spot, a bright orange gash giving way to a muddy brown, has grown slowly, inexorably wider. It is with some dismay that you find that your body has kept pace with that rust spot.

The rust spot seems symbolic, somehow, of the slow decay and decline of the Vet. It's not that old. Not really. Thirty-two? Don't some of us have socks older than that?

It was hailed as state-of-the-art when it and its cookie-cutter replicas in Pittsburgh (Three Rivers Stadium) and in Cincinnati (Riverfront Stadium) opened to great fanfare. Such innovation. A facility in which you could play both football and baseball. Imagine that. What do you suppose they'll think of next?

But they have outlived their usefulness and have been allowed to fall into neglect. Playing two sports in the same stadium has fallen out of favor.

And now, all three are either going or are already gone.

Here, the goodbyes will begin tomorrow.

The last regular-season Eagles game.

Oh, the Birds still should have a couple of playoff games, and then there will be an entire Phillies season to get through, although for a change that is not nearly the dismal prospect it has been in most of the last decade and a half. But the Vet's time is at hand. Its handsome successor as the aerie for the Eagles is already part of the city's skyline. Only an Irishman who is a hopeless romantic could choke on nostalgia and find a reason to mourn the passing of the Vet. Most people will dance gleefully on its grave.

But nostalgia, they say, is recalling all the fun without remembering all the pain.

You've heard all the tales by now, of the rats as big as linebackers, of a weight room seedy and laughably cramped, of ceiling tiles collapsed, of floors turned into flowing rivers by geysers from fractured plumbing, and of course, the playing surface itself, that killer carpet, shatterer of knees, destroyer of careers.

And they're true.

Jon Gruden, once the Birds' offensive coordinator, will swear to you that once, in the hours just before dawn, the ceiling above his desk gave way and into his surprised lap fell two rats and a cat. They eyed each other for a moment and then ran in four different directions.

There were times when you'd walk the corridors down in the bowels of the building and eyes would shine out at you from the shadows, and you would quicken your step, trepidation being more of a motivator than curiosity.

"Oh, damn, look at that one!" Ray Rhodes shouted one time as an enormous rat scuttled past.

"You could put a saddle on that and ride it in the rodeo," the former head coach said, awe in his voice.

The Vet had its moments, though.

You saw The Great Wallenda walk across the rim of the Vet on a high wire, and no one exhaled until he was on the other side. And you saw Kite-man misjudge his landing and crash into the center-field wall. He was booed, of course.

You saw the Dallas Cowboys and Jimmy Johnson's unmoving pom-padour pelted with ice missiles as they ran for locker room sanctuary.

You saw Jaworski to Quick, over the middle, 99 yards in overtime, and you saw the 76ers' championship parade end out around the 50-yard line in glorious June sunshine.

You saw Tug McGraw throw strike three past Willie Wilson on a World Series night as tart as apple cider.

You saw Army–Navy do glorious battle and then, the blood and mud smeared on them, stand at attention and salute each other in the December gloaming while the cannon fire thundered and the alma maters of each academy were played. It is not possible to look upon such a moment and not be moved to your core.

You wrote thousands—no, tens of thousands—of words, typing with fingers stiff and numb from the cold, sitting on plastic swivel chairs as inviting as a polar ice cap, while icicles formed on the baseboard heater.

And you got stuck in that walk-in closet of an elevator so many times you considered getting your mail there.

You saw goats and heroes and witnessed acts of wondrous valor and unfathomable stupidity.

You saw more losses than wins. You saw whole sections stand and, as one, spell out: E-A-G-L-E-S! Such passion. Such loyalty.

In your mind, you still see Wilbert Montgomery, on a day of incredible cold, with some of the green faces bare to the waist, busting off tackle and running into the end zone and right on into the only Super Bowl the franchise has ever played in. The stadium can be brought down, the concrete can be vaporized, the rubble replaced by a parking lot.

But the memories, ah, they are what will endure.

Vet II: It Was Made for Us

A dump. He called it a dump.

Jeffrey Lurie, the owner of the Eagles, called Veterans Stadium, the arena in which his very own team plays all of its home games, a dump.

He is right, of course. But he misses the essential point, which is the Philadelphia point, which is: Yes, it is a dump, but it is *our* dump.

And for all its inhospitable and cheerless cold, for all its crumbling concrete and flaking paint, for all its leaks and stark lack of architectural soul, for all its dank, foreboding gothic grimness, it has, throughout its 32-year-old life, served a most useful, if vaguely ignoble, purpose.

It has redefined what is meant by home-field advantage.

Because opponents would sooner play in the Black Hole of Calcutta.

And the Eagles will tell you that the Vet is worth points. Yes, sir. At least a field goal. More if the playing surface is as slick as an ice floe and the seams frayed and the sinkholes collapsing.

Even now, the Tampa Bay Buccaneers, who will fill out the marquee for the very last football game to be played at the Vet, are trying to psych themselves, trying to convince themselves that the stadium in which they have gone down with barely a whimper of protest in their last three visits will not be the wind-lashed turf of treachery that they have come to know and dread and loathe. Or that the fans, those passion-frothed zealots, knowing that this is the stadium's football valedictory, will be passive and sedate. And silent. Ha! A forest of howler monkeys will sound muted compared to the showers of sound that even now are building.

So then, a dump it is, yes. The Vet is This Old House of football, but without any of the fixing up. It is quintessential Philadelphia, like the current team in residence—hard and unyielding and gritty, without pretense or airs.

Aesthetically, it may have all the charm of a Port-a-Potty, but it has been an ally and an asset as well.

And now its end is near, and how fitting if its last hurrah were to be the victory that propels the Eagles into the Super Bowl.

As a franchise, the Birds have treated the Vet as a family skeleton loosed from the closet. They have done nothing to commemorate it, or all that was done there. Fixated on their new stadium, they have turned their back on the Vet, pretending either that it never existed or that it isn't worth remembering.

Pity.

For as quarterback Donovan McNabb noted yesterday: "Some guys did some pretty miraculous things there."

Yes. Yes, they did.

Oh, there were more games lost there than won. But there were heroic deeds done there, too. If it wasn't a field of dreams, it was a field of memories.

And that's what will survive.

It is also to be fervently hoped that the Vet itself will survive Sunday, that either in anguished defeat or in ecstatic victory, the fans will not turn into souvenir scavengers. The Vet still has life, after all, and a purpose.

The debate about the specifics of its demise goes on—the dusty pyrotechnics of implosion or the brutish, no-frills assault of the wrecking ball?

Meanwhile, the Phillies have an entire season left, 81 games to be devoted to the relentless merchandising of nostalgia. Their very last home game, September 28th, a Sunday, sold out in about 37 seconds.

So, while the Eagles may regard the Vet as a place they cannot flee fast enough, and want to scrub from their memory banks, the Phillies have taken exactly the opposite tack. Their summer will be one long Irish wake, spent in celebration, not mourning. Of course, the Phillies also hold the deed and the title to all the furniture and knickknacks, which will be auctioned off in assorted ways. The Eagles may see nothing of value in remembering the Vet, but the Phillies see something worth resurrecting and recalling, and, yes, turned into a memorabilia buck or two. Nothing wrong with a little creative commerce.

And there will be a market for those bones.

People will buy a seat for the family den. Or a swatch of rug for the mantel. They are artifacts that will stir memories. And the irony is, the Vet may turn out to be more valuable in death than it was in life. Like most of us, it is apt to be remembered more fondly as the years go by. Time has a way of softening.

Ryan Howard: A New Hero . . . Just in Time

SEPTEMBER 6, 2006

At the plate, he paws at the dirt, takes root like an oak and, holding the bat like Thor's hammer, points it, one-handed, out toward some distant dot on the horizon, where soon he will mash yet another home run.

In Philadelphia, where we gleefully eat our own, a new hero is on the ascent. Ryan James Howard is his name, and swatting pitched balls jaw-dropping distances is his game.

He has elevated himself right up there on the town's marquee alongside Allen Iverson, the Little Big Man, and Donovan McNabb, to whom is entrusted the care and feeding of the city's hottest passion.

The Phillies have been committing baseball for 123 years, and by their reckoning, in that span 1,780 different players have worn the Fightin's colors, and none of them ever stroked as many homers in one season as Howard has in this one.

His total stands at 53. That is five more than the previous franchise record, struck by the elegant and occasionally effortless Michael Jack Schmidt, who played the game as though wearing a tuxedo and top hat.

Like Schmidt, Howard's swing is compact, thus increasing his margin for error. Nor does it hurt that, at six-feet-two and 252 pounds, he is stronger than garlic. Schmidt himself has graciously acknowledged Howard to be a more accomplished and knowledgeable hitter than Schmidt was at this point in his career.

In only his second season in the major leagues, Howard demonstrates an uncommon understanding of how opponents will pitch him. And in baseball, you continually adjust and adapt, or else you are returned to a seat in the bus that is the transport through the bush leagues.

What is appealing about Howard is his demeanor and emotional equilibrium. The town lavishes its affections on him now, with standing ovations, with we-are-not-worthy bowing, with urgent chants of "MVP! MVP!" Intoxicating stuff, and even more so if you are only 26.

But there has not been a hint of the prima donna about him, none of the pouting petulance of, say, Barry Bonds, whose pursuit of Henry Aaron's career home–run record has deteriorated into a joyless, boo-filled odyssey of tedium that is not going to be realized this season.

Howard's self-celebrations have been muted, limited mostly to a broad, engaging grin. He is right to be subdued because this is, after all, Philadelphia, where we have a way of erecting pedestals and then promptly converting them into gallows.

For example, in last Friday's *Inquirer,* the Philly.com poll asked the populace its expectations for Howard, and 46 percent of the respondents said: "This is it. After this year, he will fade into an average hitter."

That lyric from *New York, New York,* the one that goes, "If I can make it here, I can make it anywhere"? Wrong city.

What should sustain Howard is that, unlike most one-dimensional power hitters, he is also hitting for average, hovering around .300, which is the eternal line of demarcation between respectability and Hot Damn!

We're running low on heroes at the moment, not only in Philadelphia but in all of Sports World. Waves of scandal wash over us and there is a persistent, gnawing sense of innocence lost. The very day my piece ran extolling the ferocity of the human spirit as exemplified by the cyclist Floyd Landis in winning the Tour de France, it was announced that he had failed the drug test.

The blog whisperers already are asking: Is Howard juiced? Such is life these days, where presumption of guilt rules, where shadows of suspicion hang like a shroud over each new feat.

All is not lost, however. There are still some deserving of our admiration. There is the golfer Eldrick Woods, who took off half the summer to mourn the death of his father/mentor and now has won five consecutive tournaments, 53 in all, a dozen of those majors. All this and he is only 30, and just in his 10th year as a pro.

Tiger Woods' mental ferocity is matched only by his thermonuclear driver. For those of us who grew up and grew old awaiting the equal of Jack Nicklaus, it is no longer blasphemy to pronounce him here.

And then there is Joseph Vincent Paterno, ruler of Happy Valley, almost 80, and most assuredly not juiced. Penn State won its opener Saturday. The coach prowled the sidelines as always, cuffs rolled up, refusing to wear a hat despite an insistent drizzle. On his last visit to the doctor, he related, he was told he could coach for 10 more years.

He saw the doc because his leg hurt after he had scaled Mount Nittany with his grandchildren. Almost 80 and still climbing mountains . . . could there be anything more symbolic?

Never-Say-Die Phillies

OCTOBER 2, 2007

Friday night, wedding reception, Blue Bell: Six men run discreet relays from the ballroom to the TV set, returning with updates of the Phillies and Mets games. Their reports are delivered with gleeful chortling, in acerbic shorthand: "Fightin's up 3, choking New York dogs down 4." The bride dances with her father, and everyone smiles, and the good news is whispered: Phillies inching closer to first place.

Saturday, gym: The TV sets are zeroed in on the first-place Phillies. The man on the treadmill next to me squints and asks: "What's that Mets score? I can't read it." The Mets have two touchdowns and an extra point. The man yelps in anguish: "Whaaaaaat" and shoots off the back of his treadmill. He sits, ruefully, and mutters: "I knew it was too good to be true." Obviously, a lifelong Phillies fan.

Sunday, checkout line: A beefy man with the tentacles of his radio elbow-deep into his ears suddenly bellows: "Rollins is on." Grins all around. Comes another bellow: "Rollins stole second." Happy nodding of heads. Soon: "Rollins stole third." Now there is growing applause. Then: "He just scored. . . . Phillies are ahead." An impromptu chorus: M-V-P. . . M-V-P!

So went a weekend for the memory bank, three days of golden splendor and apple-cider nights, of lighted candles and frenzied helicoptering of white rally towels, all courtesy of a Major League Baseball team whose mottled history is mostly one of angst and frustration.

Ah, but not this time, my friend. Not this time. No, this time the Fightin's are truly worthy of their nickname, and none of that usual sneering derision either. This is all guts and glory.

They won their division with a trumpets-blaring stretch run that was made even sweeter because it involved an inglorious free-fall, flame-out death spiral by the New York Mets, who are to the Phillies roughly what Dallas is to the Eagles.

In the "Season of the 10,000 Losses," for a franchise that has suffered more defeats than any professional team in any sport, ever, the Phillies have achieved Deliverance. For only the 10th time in their 125-year history, they will play beyond the regular schedule.

And they will do so with the full-throated accompaniment of a city whose yearning for a champion goes back generations and cuts clean to the bone.

Sport is the great common denominator. It is the umbilical that ties us to one another. It cuts across all the mean and petty lines, transcends the unspoken boundaries, and has no regard for gender, race or age.

Being a fan requires no more than a simple emotional investment. But beware, for over time it will grow and swell and inflame and rouse from you a passion you never knew existed.

Most of the time, the Phillies have tantalized you, seduced you, left you in gnashing rage or weeping sorrow. But this is a team meant for this town and for this time. This is a team that does not swoon, that does not go gentle into that good night.

Of its 89 wins, 48 were achieved when they had to come from behind.

"Not an ounce of give-up in 'em," says manager Charlie Manuel, who knows a little bit about not giving up, having survived cancer and a heart attack, among other triumphs.

Says Jayson Werth, a platoon player: "We don't feel like we're out of a game. It's been crazy. Nothing can surprise us."

Crazy, yes. But a delicious lunacy. How many school-night bedtimes were fudged, or just plain ignored, during the month of September? Here is the rationalization for being allowed to stay up waiting for one more rally: The Fightin's have provided a life lesson, applicable for any and every age. Never give in, never give up. Never. Ever. Never.

They were seven games behind with 17 to play. They won 13, equaling the biggest September comeback in major league history. And the Mets, well, in a delightful bit of irony, the Mets did a passable impersonation of the Phillies' Great Collapse of 1964.

And the '07 Phillies did all of this in spite of a crippling, season-long run of injuries. Their disabled list was as thick as a Manhattan phone book. Asked how this team was held together, Jimmy Rollins replied: "Motrin and duct tape."

Also held together by Manuel, who gave a determined demonstration of placid, panic-free managing, and by Rollins, who played every game and scored more runs than anyone else in the National League, and in the process was without peer at his position.

In the euphoria of Sunday's win, Ryan Howard, last year's MVP, leaned into a camera and, with an appealing touch of class, said: "I gladly relinquish my title to this man. He deserves it."

Yes, he does.

It was Rollins who first uttered the words "We're the team to beat" back in January. It was not said in arrogance or cocky posing, but rather as an honest, if opinionated, assessment. In Game 162, it became reality.

This team has caught many by surprise. We have become accustomed to oh-so-close. We have come to expect being led to Lover's Leap, and then pushed. Ah, but you have heard all of this a thousand times and more by now, about curses and negativity, hexes and terminal pessimism, the shroud that cloaks our town.

But perhaps it has never been quite as bad as we think. Listen, for example, to Pat Burrell. Pat the Bat rallied from a horrid first half of the season and ended with 30 home runs and 97 RBI—respectable numbers, indeed. But in his stay here, he has been roundly roasted. And yet . . . and yet, well, listen: "It's always been good to be a Phillie. Even the bad times have been great."

There is something to be learned from such a stalwart sentiment.

So now what? Well, now comes a thing to which we are unaccustomed: Tomorrow. The Fightin's are going to play October baseball. At home. They are in the playoffs.

And in the words of their beloved Dirt Ball, Chase Utley: "Once you're in, anything can happen."

And so it can.

And so it can.

Day of Destiny

Forty-four years. That's how long we've kept the candle in the window. Forty-four years since the Eagles last won the championship of professional football.

Forty-four years.

Six hundred ninety-two games. Eleven coaches. Five owners.

Forty-four years.

Sons have become fathers, and fathers have become grandfathers. Women have married and had babies, and those babies have had babies.

Forty-four years.

And now the Birds are teasingly, tantalizingly, enticingly, seductively close. All that lies between them and victory in Super Bowl XXXIX is a lionhearted opponent that exhibits clinical precision and has unshakable confidence.

This is familiar ground for the New England Patriots, who almost never lose and who are seeking their third triumph in this game in the last four years. Theirs is the stuff of dynasty.

But the Eagles have sailed through the chaos of Circus Maximus this week with impressive aplomb. They do not seem cowed in any way. Nor should they be. Though they remain one-touchdown underdogs, they will win this game.

They will do it primarily with their carnivorous defense, which yielded fewer points than nearly any other in the NFL.

They will do it by prizing every possession and by not committing turnovers as Donovan McNabb, who finally gets to play the big room, manages the game adroitly and cashes in every scoring opportunity.

They will do it by not hobbling themselves with penalties and by not being in awe of a most imposing opponent.

They will, in short, need to play flawless football.

They are capable of that.

It should be a corking good game. These teams have been the best in the league for a long stretch. And while it is the Patriots who keep coming back to this game, it's not as though they have won their two titles by lopsided margins. In fact, both of their Super Bowl wins were the result of last-gasp field goals.

Boston and New England, as you may have heard, are on quite a roll, having in the last year won a Super Bowl and then ended an 86-year journey through the desert by taking a World Series. Tacking on another Super Bowl victory would be on the piggish side.

Hopeful Iggles loyalists have tried to suggest that the Red Sox's Series victory is a favorable omen for Philadelphia, which has been without a parade for 22 years, a span covering 86 separate major pro–sports seasons. We are, indeed, overdue, but simply being overdue does not take the place of bone-splintering tackling and jump-over-the-moon pass-catching.

And, yes, Terrell Owens, catcher of passes and controversy and an astonishingly rapid healer, will play. The suspicion here is that he will be used when the Birds are near the end zone and he can climb an invisible ladder to haul in lobs. He will become an instant folk hero in the Olde Towne.

The game will also offer an intriguing coaching matchup.

The Patriots are under the direction of Bill Belichick, whose usual attire is a hooded sweatshirt the color of ashes. The hood looks rather like a monk's cowl and offers only the occasional glimpse of the coach's face, which is invariably scrunched in concentration as he devises some new bit of genius.

Belichick has lost only one of 10 playoff games. He is tied in that regard with the sainted Vince Lombardi. His approach is to first take away the opponent's best weapon or preference. This is usually done with an assassin's cool.

The Birds are where Andy Reid said they would be when he took their coaching job half a dozen years ago, though they certainly have not gotten here without travail and torment that has become the stuff of legend.

Reid wears Ben Franklin–style spectacles and covers his mouth with the game plan. He has improved in the area of adjusting on the go. There was a time when the Birds seemed to be outcoached every week. Now you hardly ever hear that.

The Birds' defense must beat Tom Brady, a quarterback who is merely 8-0 in postseason starts. Jim Johnson, the Merlin of defensive coordinators, has waited a lifetime to get to this game. You presume this will be his masterpiece.

On offense, the difference will be Brian Westbrook. As runner, receiver and returner, somewhere, somehow, he will end up matched against someone slower and less agile. He will end up in the end zone.

I make it 24-20, Eagles.

The parade will be Tuesday.

We will discover, to our great pleasure, that we haven't forgotten how to do it.

Eagles: We Wait,
Starting Over . . . Again

FEBRUARY 7, 2005

Us again, huh? Another tease. Another punch in the mouth.

For a lifetime we have been waiting for these seven words: The Eagles have won the Super Bowl.

So we'll wait a while longer. But that's OK. That's all right. We're good at waiting, and enduring.

On a clear, crisp night in a cavernous stadium just inside the Florida–Georgia border, the two best teams in the NFL whaled away at each other for close to four hours, and it ended with the Eagles one brick shy of a load.

Philadelphia Eagles 21, dynasty-in-the-making New England Patriots 24. So close. So excruciatingly close.

So the parade will be put on hold. Again. The Birds will come back down the mountain and regroup and give it another go.

And when you're over the ache, when the mourning is done with, when the numbness finally goes away, this consolation remains: The Eagles will be back here again. Soon. As soon as the next Supe, perhaps. They are young, they return the nucleus of their team, they are well stocked for the coming draft, and they adroitly manage the salary cap.

They remain comfortably ahead of their competition in the NFC and surely will be ranked number one in that conference at the start of the next season. And now they know exactly what is required to win a Super Bowl.

"The guys have got a taste of it now," said coach Andy Reid. "I'm sure they'll want to come back."

"This was still a successful year," said quarterback Donovan McNabb. "I'm going to continue to hold my head high. We'll be back."

They keep creeping closer. They finally got over the can't-win-the-big-one obstacle by winning the NFC title game after three years of failure. Now only The Big One remains.

In their first appearance in The Big One since 1981, they did not play well. They were unable to run with any effectiveness. Their passing game was tepid. Their defense was OK, but more than OK was needed.

More than anything, though, what doomed the Birds was crippling carelessness with the football. They committed four turnovers, including three McNabb interceptions. Good football teams will make you pay for those mistakes. Great football teams will bury you.

The Patriots are three-time champions because turnovers, and cashing them in, are at the core of what drives the Patriots.

Terrell Owens, who was center ring all week of Circus Maximus, started for the Birds, and promptly caught a pass on the second play of the game. Before he was done, he would have eight more receptions for 122 yards in all—a remarkable performance for someone whose leg is held together by stuff from a bin in a hardware store.

But none of the other Birds could match that productivity.

"They were able to come up with the big play when they needed it," said McNabb, "and we weren't."

Sometimes, the game really is that simple.

Eagles loyalists, as boisterous and passionate as always, seemed to outnumber Patriots partisans all week in public gatherings, sometimes by margins of 10-1, and on game night they turned Alltel Stadium into an echo chamber for their frenzied spelling bees: E-A-G-L-...

The Birds were making the pilgrimage to the NFL's Holy Land for the first time in 24 years while New England was in the Supe for the third time in four years, so perhaps the novelty had worn off for Patriots fans. But not for Birds boosters. No sir. The wait for a parade felt interminable. And when the Birds scored, the Eagles fight song was sung thunderously and, it seemed, by almost everyone in the arena. It amounted to a home-field advantage.

The game had no rhythm, lurching along at an uneven pace due to injuries, reviews of challenged calls and other delays, not the least of which was commercial after commercial.

Neither team could sustain anything, until the Eagles finally stitched together an impressive 81-yard drive that ended with tight end L.J. Smith hand-fighting his way away from clutching linebacker Roman Phifer in the end zone and squeezing Donovan McNabb's bullet pass.

It was amazing. McNabb had been sacked three times, the Eagles had committed two turnovers and very nearly two more, and yet here they were in the lead. The game is not supposed to work that way. Maybe it was a favorable omen, but of course it's hazardous living on the edge that way.

McNabb did rally the Birds and it was 24-21 Patriots, inside the final two minutes. If the Birds could recover the onside kick, well, there's never been an overtime in the Super Bowl.

There still hasn't been. McNabb's third interception and the Birds' fourth turnover of the game, in the closing seconds, sealed it.

"We'll be back," McNabb repeated.

There is every reason to think they will be.

2

Baseball . . .
Around the Horn

Managers: "I Managed Good
But They Played Bad"

MARCH 21, 2008

When Bobby Bragan replaced Birdie Tebbetts as manager of the Milwaukee Braves in 1963, he opened his desk drawer to find two envelopes marked number one and number two. Taped to them was this note from Tebbetts to his successor: "Open only in emergencies."

By Bragan's second season, the Braves had not only failed to improve, they were worse than ever. At wit's end, Bragan opened the first envelope and found this message: "Blame it on me." The team continued to fall like a stone down a well. Desperate, Bragan opened envelope number two to find this: "Prepare two envelopes."

Earl Weaver, the acerbic bantam rooster who managed the Baltimore Orioles to sustained success, was lecturing the elegant Jim Palmer about the fine art of pitching. Palmer listened for a time and then said imperiously: "Earl, all you know about major league pitching is that you couldn't hit it."

For the 11 seasons that Casey Stengel managed the Yankees, they won no fewer than 92 games each year. Not to mention seven World Series. He had such players as DiMaggio, Mantle, Berra, Rizzuto, Martin and Ford. He moved to the other side of New York and led the woebegone expansion Mets to a 175-404 record, and was moved to utter this mournful wail: "Can't anybody here play this game?"

Baseball involves a lot of luck, Stengel was told consolingly. Yes, he is said to have agreed, it's bad luck not to have good players.

In the late 1990s, the Phillies had a young and not very good—OK, bad—team. It was decided to bring in a manager who would bring along patience, tolerance and forbearance. Translation: Feed them, burp them, change them.

Terry Francona, who is a genuinely good man and true, soldiered on without complaint. Admirable, but unappreciated. In four years, the Fightin's played like the Faintin's—78 games under .500, and rarely competitive. The whole mess was laid at Francona's feet.

The Boston Red Sox, fabled in song and legend for their lead role in their long-running, star-crossed Shakespearean tragedy, saw what had escaped so many in Philadelphia. As you may have heard, Boston, with maestro Francona wielding the baton, won a World Series. And then another. Francona, denigrated in these precincts as such a clueless dolt, just signed a fat extension.

Sometimes, justice really is served.

There are more thankless jobs out there than that of baseball manager. Batting cleanup behind the elephants in the circus parade comes to mind.

The problem is, in no other sport are there so many who are convinced they know so much. Certainly more than that fathead skipper we've got—grumble, grumble, grumble.

The opportunities for second-guessing are so much more plentiful. In football, there might be 80 snaps to question. In basketball, the pace of play is too fast, too unstructured, to analyze every possession. In hockey, well, no one ever sees the puck actually go in the net anyway. Ah, but in baseball, 200 pitches are there for the taking. Not to mention all the bonehead tactical gaffes—the double switch, the pinch hit, the bullpen juggling, to sacrifice or not to sacrifice . . . on and on and on.

We know, don't we? We know. We all know.

Or, at least, we think we do.

The debate is endless, and forever unresolved, and it is this: How big a role does the manager really play? How many games does he lose a year? Or win? On this, everyone has an opinion. And most of them are not the same.

Once, the managerial style in vogue was that of the demanding despot, a ranting little pepper pot to goad the boys along: John McGraw, Gene Mauch, Leo Durocher, Billy Martin.

Now, the trend is toward sitter and soother. The Tommy Lasorda school of stroke-stroke-stroke: Joe Torre, Bobby Cox. Or Sparky Anderson, alias Captain Hook of Cincinnati's Big Red Machine of the mid-1970s: "You take a guy out for a pinch-hitter, he ain't gonna be your friend."

Larry Bowa, hired by the Phillies to shake things up and, in an all-too-familiar scenario, later let go because shake-up fell out of favor, had this to say: "The players today, they're s-o-o-o-o sensitive."

Of all the managerial records—for that matter, of all the records in sports—there is one absolutely, positively that is beyond catching: No one anywhere—repeat, anybody, anywhere, anytime—is going to match the numbers of Cornelius McGillicuddy.

Connie Mack managed in the major leagues for 53 years. The last 50 were in Philadelphia. Fittingly, considering our luckless civic history, his A's teams lost more than they won. When he retired, in 1950, he was 87.

Unlike all the rest, he was never in danger of being fired. He had the ultimate protection possible—he owned the team.

Right Fielders:
Write If You Get Work

MARCH 22, 2008

In the beginning, it is Devil's Island.

It is a place of exile. It is where you station the fat kid. Or the one with glasses. And then you hope no one hits a ball out there. The kid himself hopes so even more fervently than you. Prayer is very big in position number nine.

But as you move up in competition, right field begins to assume importance and cachet and glamour. It has become, by tradition, one of the Big Stick positions, a place to stash one of your most robust hitters.

Number nine frequently bats number three, number four or number five in the order. The prototype number nine hits for average and for power—say .330, with 50 doubles, 30 homers, 100 driven in, 100 scored. And defensively, well, those days of his exile are long gone.

Now you want to will the ball to be hit to your right fielder because, at the highest level, he is armed. That is a .357 Magnum hanging from his shoulder, and he loves to show it off. Go ahead, punk, make my day. Try to run on me.

There are four basic opportunities for number nine to trot out his gun. The first is based on deception—loafing in on the ball, feigning disinterest and nonchalance, then throwing to first base behind the runner, who, if nailed, will hear about it. Often. From both benches.

Then there is the charge-it, crow-hop, bada-bing laser to second—the throw that reduces a double into another embarrassing out.

The third is the one that goes to third. It is the longest and deepest throw of them all and usually is delivered on one hissing bounce. This is the intercontinental ballistic missile of baseball throws, with the third baseman grinning in anticipation while waving the ball at the runner who knows, too late, that he is cooked meat.

The fourth is the throw home. Number nine uses the first baseman as his sight line, cranks and fires. When all the parts work, the catcher instructs the first baseman to let the ball through. To bounce or throw it all the way on the fly is optional. The main thing is to get it there—the sooner it arrives the better, for the catcher is bracing himself and is about to try to put the tag on a runaway freight train.

Speed helps at position number nine, though it is not as crucial as in center field. But even if lacking, it can be offset by anticipation, by doing outfield homework, by putting in the time to learn the quirks and geometry of the ricochets and caroms of the various ballparks, where the ball is apt to go and how best to get to it.

In the roll call of right-field arenas noted for their distinctive features, perhaps the most memorable was the original Yankee Stadium, the epitome of home–field advantage. It was less than 300 feet to the right-field fence. Pop flies turned into home runs. So the Yanks loaded up on left–handed pull hitters and thus were born the Bronx Bombers.

While Fenway is best known for its Green Monster, the right-field corner is only 302 feet from home plate, but there is a sharp, sudden jut-out and by the time the ball reaches center field, it's 380 feet to home.

In Philadelphia, when the A's played in Shibe Park, they put up a 12-foot fence intended to discourage free viewing by the great unwashed. The masses got around that by climbing up on rooftops. The A's responded by tacking a 22-foot-high fence on top of the 12 feet. It came to be known, of course, as the Spite Fence.

And on the subject of dimensions, what about your right fielder? Must he be cheetah-sleek, all streamlined and svelte? Not necessarily. The greatest baseball player of all time put in time at number nine, and also, on occasion, at number seven. He was a squatty-body with a ponderous, beerfed torso that was perched atop matchstick legs. He ran in a peculiar, mincing, pigeon-toed gait, but one that he could convert into a higher gear—he stole 123 bases in his matchless career.

Somehow he always seemed to get to the ball. His fielding average was over 97 percent five times, more than 98 percent another. And one season he led all players at his position with a .996 mark. That position happened to be number one. He was pitching for the Boston Red Sox at the time, and his left–handed deliveries left the American League hitters flailing futilely—in 1916, he went 23-12 with a 1.75 ERA, and in 1917, he was 24-13 with a 2.01 ERA. And, oh yes, hit .325.

When he was sent to the Yankees, he was switched to number nine. Incredibly, there were those who forecast that it was a shift to be rued and lamented for all time. For his future, it was argued, was on the mound, and not to shine as a number nine.

So whatever became of that George Herman Ruth fellow, anyway?

Center Fielders:
Green Acres

MARCH 23, 2008

When the Phillies won their one and only World Series, center field was patrolled by a ground-gulping greyhound whose range seemed without limit, so much so that it was said of him: "Seventy-five percent of the Earth is covered by water and the other 25 percent is covered by Garry Maddox."

And so it was, from sea to shining sea. Or at least from foul line to foul line. Those who played left field and right field alongside Maddox soon learned that the correct reaction to any ball, any ball, hit their way was to chirp encouragingly: "Lotta room, Garry Lee, lotta room."

Position number eight is for ballet. If Baryshnikov played baseball, he would be the center fielder. Minus the tights, of course.

Position number eight is where they glide over those green, manicured pastures with such loping, easy elegance and grace that poets weep. And where they scale the outfield walls like mountain goats tiptoeing along cliff edges. And where, in a froth, they mount a hell-bent-for-leather, storm-the-beaches, belly-sliding sellout, plucking the ball off the grass, and holding aloft in triumph the resulting snow cone.

Even today, the signature play of position number eight remains frozen in grainy black-and-white: Willie Mays pursuing Vic Wertz's mighty smash across three time zones in the 1954 World Series, running it down in deepest center, turning and whirling and unleashing it like a discus thrower corkscrewing himself into the ground.

Of Mays it was said, with hushed reverence: "Where he plays is where triples go to die." That is the essence of position number eight.

And where Joe DiMaggio played, ah, that was sacred sod, indeed. Or at least that is what my grandfather told me the first time we drove to Chicago, long before the interstate, for a Sunday doubleheader: ChiSox vs. Bronx Bombers.

"Watch the center fielder," he said. "He is liquid. He flows."

In the golden age of position number eight, there were three teams in New York, each possessing a wondrous center fielder: Mays, the incomparable Giant who owned the Polo Grounds and Coogan's Bluff; Mickey Mantle, the Yankee, the best one-legged player you ever saw, all power and speed and injuries and tragic flaws; and the Brooklyn Dodgers' Duke

Snider, the Lord of Flatbush, with a sweet, sweet swing, laboring in the immense shadows cast by the first two.

They made a song about them, a paean to nostalgia: "Willie, Mickey and the Duke."

Here, the Phillies have had their share of worthy number eights. The late Richie Ashburn, with that wry, dry, delightful sense of humor. To the growling frustration of the pitcher, he could foul off two dozen offerings before slapping one into the hole.

And then there was The Dude. Pig Pen himself. Unsanitary, yes, but a killer competitor. Leonard Kyle Dykstra was the perfect leadoff hitter, patient and oddly disciplined considering his lack of discipline anywhere off the field. He left clumps of his chewing tobacco all over position number eight, and other center fielders went after batted balls in his area as though picking their way through a field of dog droppings.

Most recently, and for far too short a time, there was Aaron Rowand, who literally broke his face on the center-field wall of the new ballpark. That, of course, instantly endeared him to Phillies fans, who dote on effort.

"I thought that's the way you're supposed to play," he said.

And so it is.

Left Fielders:
Out in the Great Beyond

MARCH 24, 2008

L eft field is baseball's Witness Protection Program.

The idea is to encourage your man to wreak as much incriminating havoc as possible and then ship him into hiding, secreted well out of the field of play. Traditionally, left field has been where you sacrifice pyrotechnic offense in exchange for late-inning, lock-down defense. You want position number seven to get you ahead with his bat but without giving him a chance to lose it with his glove.

Number seven does not require the foot speed of a number eight, nor the howitzer arm of a number nine. The throws are shorter, the acreage to be covered smaller. The double switch seems made for a number seven, you'd think.

In the 1978 NL playoffs, Phillies manager Danny Ozark, in a moment of unfathomable and costly negligence, forgot to remove his number seven, the power-hitting but slow-footed Greg Luzinski, while nursing a lead late. Sure enough, a ball that would have been inhaled by his usual replacement clanked off The Bull's glove. The Phils lost. Ozark: My bad.

Nowhere in the manual does it specify that number seven should be insufferable, arrogant, profane, boorish and, generally, about as cuddly as a cactus. Perhaps it is only coincidence that many of the greatest number sevens have been as obnoxious as they were talented.

Start with Rickey ("Today I am the greatest of all time") Henderson. The numbers—bases stolen, walks coaxed, runs scored—are unmatched and argue that he is the greatest leadoff hitter of all time. And if you don't believe so, just ask him. Peacock proud, he milked each at-bat shamelessly—posing, posturing, preening. But he could manufacture a run all by himself, without benefit of even a single hit.

Then there was Ted Williams, who wanted to be able to walk down the street and hear a passerby whisper: "There goes the greatest hitter of all time."

He very well might be. He was the last to hit .400, and might hold that distinction forever. His defense improved with time—he became accustomed to the quirks and foibles of the Green Monster, that celebrated, 37-foot-high, left-field wall in Fenway.

There were those who thought him less than enthusiastic in his pursuit of batted balls, and he frequently saluted them with one-half of the peace sign, delivered emphatically and with undisguised relish. The Splendid Spitter also spat at them with gusto. Thumping Theodore was no candidate for the diplomatic corps. He had an even lower opinion of the media, which, in the considered opinion of some, should be counted as an asset rather than a shortcoming.

Clearly, the most controversial position number seven of all time is Barry Bonds. And he may only be warming up. And merely mentioning his name is enough. For now.

The preceding evidence aside, it is possible to be a gentleman and shine in left, the most prominent example being Stan Musial, he of the coiled peek-a-boo stance, the lightning-bolt bat and the impeccable demeanor.

Like Babe Ruth, he began as a left–handed pitcher. Ruth's bat helped persuade the Yankees to make him an everyday performer. Musial had to switch to left field after injuring his money shoulder. All he did was average .331 over 22 seasons while collecting 3,630 hits, second most in National League history. And he was unfailingly the gentleman, on the field and off. Long, long before the birth of that insipid "You da man," Musial was known as Stan the Man.

For all the right reasons.

Shortstops:
The Acrobats

MARCH 25, 2008

He looked as if he had been put together with leftover parts, so bow-legged that his legs resembled croquet wickets, his arms so long he could, they say, tie his shoes standing up. His feet were 14s.

But somehow, despite all that ungainliness, Honus Wagner, the first of the great shortstops, possessed uncommon range, often roaming well behind third to snare a ground ball. And then the fun began. His enormous hands were said to be shovels, and when he picked up the ball, he also picked up gravel, pebbles and assorted flotsam and jetsam, all of which were delivered to the first baseman, who braced himself to catch what sounded like a hailstorm on a tin roof.

Wagner was the first to prove a shortstop needn't be strictly a glove man. Playing in Pittsburgh the first two decades of the 20th century, he won eight National League batting titles. A young Christy Mathewson asked his catcher what was Wagner's weakness, and the catcher replied: "A base on balls."

Just as Wagner's range defied logic or easy explanation, there is no set blueprint for building a shortstop.

They may be diminutive—little men whose size earned them self-evident nicknames: Phil "Scooter" Rizzuto or Pee Wee Reese. They had happy feet and flitted about the infield like moths dancing in and out of the light, and at bat they made pests of themselves while leading off or dropping down a bunt. That's right, a bunt. For reference, consult your history books. (A pause here while the gentlemen in attendance remove their hats and we observe a moment of silence for the passing of that undervalued and underappreciated offensive tactic, the bunt.)

Around the middle of the last century there rose a relentlessly happy warrior who combined the best of both worlds for a number six—he inhaled balls hit to the left side of the infield, and when his turn in the order came round, the outfielders were ordered back. Back. No, not far enough yet. That's right, keep going.

Ernie Banks was five feet 11, 185 pounds, neither tiny nor middle-line-backer size; just about the optimal dimensions for the ideal number six. He was lean and fluid, had a boardinghouse reach, and thus could get to balls that seemed headed to outer pastures. And he had buggy-whip wrists that drove the ball into orbit. In 19 seasons, he clubbed 512 home runs and drove in 1,636. No other number six can come close to those numbers.

Perhaps Banks' biggest distinction was his unfailing, good-humored temperament—quite a feat considering he was employed by the Chicago Cubs. "Let's play two" became his signature. Quite a contrast to the scowling mercenaries of today.

Banks begat the Wizard of Oz. Ozzie Smith began each game in the field with a child's exuberance. You could not help but smile.

Smith played shortstop, not on grass or fake turf, but as though he was on a trampoline. It is the opinion of many that he was the greatest defensive number six of them all, whose magician's glove was every bit as important as a slugger's bat. In 19 seasons, his batting average was only .262, and he drove in only 793 runs. But by the reckoning of many, he saved three times that many.

Early in his career, Cal Ripken Jr. said: "For the next 20 years, I'd like to play every inning of every game of every day." No way, the no-wayers said. For starters, he'll break down; he's too big.

He was, in fact, six feet four, 225 pounds. But the idea of a slugger playing shortstop seemed to go against all conventional baseball wisdom. So he hit 431 homers and led the league in fielding five times, and once went 95 straight games without an error. Along the way, of course, he flew past Lou Gehrig's record for consecutive games played, one of those marks thought to be uncatchable, and made it even more uncatchable. So much for conventional wisdom. So much for breaking down.

The next step in the evolution of shortstop plays in Philadelphia: in 2007, Jimmy Rollins put up numbers never before achieved by a number six, numbers good enough to win him the MVP. He has sprinter speed, potent bat, dazzling glove, cannon arm.

And he's only just begun.

Third Basemen: Duck!

Third base in one word: Incoming!

This is not a position for the faint of heart. Or the slow of reflex. Things that come at position number five do so with sizzle and hiss.

There is time to react and no time for anything else. Unless, of course, it is one of those damnable topped balls trickling down the line and you have to sprint, scoop and throw, all in the same motion—one-handed, bare-handed, underhanded. Line drives, wicked grounders, swinging bunts, cross-diamond throws of pristine accuracy and ballistic velocity— that's the fiendishly cruel and devilishly varied menu for position number five. So, the way you prepare for it is . . . is . . . ? Anyone? Yes, you in the back.

"You take a hundred infield balls, and then you take a hundred more. And a million after that."

Why, yes. Very good, Mister . . . Mister . . . ?

"Schmidt. Michael Jack Schmidt."

Of the Philadelphia Schmidts?

"Correct."

He played the position with feline grace, with such casual elegance that for much of his career the affection that should have been his all along was denied because they perceived him to be nonchalant. His fluid style was seen as lack of hustle. At last, in the twilight of his career, the fans came to understand that for all those years they had been privileged to witness genius.

The first of the celebrated third basemen was Harold Joseph Traynor, known as Pie. He blended stick and glove at what was called the Hot Corner, hitting .320 for 17 seasons at Pittsburgh in the 1920s and '30s, and posting a .947 fielding average. He drove in 1,273 runs and furthered the notion that, offensively, position number five was where you put a power guy.

Traynor was supplanted by a loose-limbed acrobat out of Baltimore whose sense of anticipation was exquisite. Brooks Robinson didn't play third—and the surrounding zip codes—as much as he vacuumed the area, sucking up balls that looked to be certain hits. Hence, Brooks Robinson was known as Hoover. Even old-timers agreed his was the slickest glove they'd seen.

The other third sacker of note was Eddie Mathews, a left–handed slugger with a physique you could strike a match on. He bombed 512 home runs and had a fielding average of .956.

Robinson was the ultimate glove, Mathews the ultimate bat, but no one ever did both as well as Schmidt. He led the league in homers eight times and he won 10 Gold Gloves and three times was MVP.

And when he retired, abruptly and without warning, and still very much a force, he did so leaving us all wanting more. He managed the trickiest part of all—he carried grace all the way to the exit.

Second Basemen:
A Full Plate

MARCH 27, 2008

Second base is where you can cheat. And get away with it.

Second being the shortest throw to first, it is accepted strategy to fudge on your positioning and move back. And back. And farther still. Second becomes more like short right field.

Position number four has to run down all those bloops and blips and assorted pop-ups and prevent them from parachuting safely, cheaply, in. Second base also has to range deep into foul territory while managing not to get run over by some slew-footed first baseman.

Second becomes the middle man in the relay throw, and the middle man in the six-to-four-to-three pitcher's best friend, and the instigator of the four-to-six-to-three other best friend. Second is also responsible for covering the bag with a runner on first and a right–handed batter up.

Second, in short, has enough to keep him from nodding off.

And, best of all, he gets to bat.

No second sacker ever did this better than Rogers Hornsby. He was, by all accounts, a taciturn loner who showed up, dialed in his usual three-for-four, and went home. Next day, same routine.

He would stand at the far corner of the batter's box—often beyond the chalk line despite the catcher's protest—and then, like a small explosion, drive into the ball.

In that gaudy, giddy decade known as the Roaring Twenties, Hornsby hit over .400 three times and over .380 three other times. His career .358 average is second only to Ty Cobb's .367. No one disputes the suggestion that he was the greatest right–handed hitter of all time.

Of all the position number fours, none endured and persevered like Jack Roosevelt Robinson. He hit .311 in a 10-year career with the Brooklyn Dodgers, and brought chaos to the base paths, daring the opponent to trap him in a rundown, and then boldly, in that peculiar pigeon-toed stride, escaping.

He burned with a consuming fire that, somehow, he managed to keep banked. He bore up against all the death threats and the profane, virulent slurs and answered the racial viciousness not by replying in kind, but by simply playing harder.

Jackie Robinson, more than any other man, changed forever the face and structure of the game. Never have so many owed such a debt to one.

One of the many who benefited from Robinson's valor was Joe Morgan, known as Little Big Man. He was only five feet seven but played with a fury in the field, and over a 22-year career drove in more than 1,100 runs.

He favored a small glove rather than the scoop shovels employed by most, explaining that it gave him a better feel for the ball. At bat, he developed a routine of flapping his arm like a chicken stretching his wings. It may have looked odd, but he accumulated more than 2,500 hits and is in the Hall of Fame.

The Phillies' current position number four is a Dirt Bag. In the best possible sense. When Chase Utley's work is done, his uniform is a rainbow of colors—blood, mud and grass, each one a testament to his impassioned work ethic.

Utley is a grinder, never giving away an at-bat, hitting for average and power with a fluid, repeating swing, and running the bases like a free safety. He is made for this town.

"The harder you play the game," he said, "the more you get out of it."

Right you are, Dirt Bag.

First Basemen:
Misunderstood

It helps to have an elastic groin. Because at first base the name of the game is s-t-r-e-t-c-h.

How far you can do the splits may be the difference between a ground ball being beaten out for a hit or one of those bang-bang, got-him-by-a-nose-hair outs.

You will also discover to your annoyance that the throws to you are sometimes one-hop bullets requiring a theatrical, sweeping snare. Fortunately, today's first-base gloves are roughly the size of Rhode Island and can flag down a large appliance. Nevertheless, feel free to add flourishes and curlicues to your performance in the never-ending struggle for appreciation of position number three.

To review, then, first base requires legs that telescope and a cobra-quick glove hand. You will also, from time to time, have to stagger around in small circles, pursuing a pop foul that has disappeared behind the sun. The opponents will make mocking noises at your obvious discomfort. Try not to let on how damnably difficult this really is.

Position number three, you see, is the most misunderstood of them all. To wit:

"We need Stretch's bat. But he's a butcher in the field. Where can we hide him?"

"First. All he has to do is catch the ball. How hard is that?"

And so the myth is passed along. Where is the love for position number three?

The most inventive nickname for a number three was affixed to Dick Stuart: Dr. Strangeglove. Yet, in a 10-season, six-team career, his fielding average was actually .982, not Gold Glove-worthy to be sure, but nowhere near as disastrous as his reputation.

And not that far behind Willie "Stretch" McCovey's .987, either. Mc-Covey was a menacing figure—he was six feet four but seemed to loom much larger, and in that regard was reminiscent of the greatest first baseman of them all, Lou Gehrig.

Combined, Stretch and the Iron Horse hit 1,014 home runs and drove in 2,550 runs. Gehrig also averaged a robust .340 lifetime. And, of course, there was also that little matter of The Streak.

One of the perks of position number three is that as a way station on the base paths, it is the ideal setting for conversational conviviality. First sackers tend to be regular Chatty Kathys who keep up a continuous dialogue, and if you're a runner who allows himself to get caught up in the talk and neglects to pay attention, well . . . zap! . . . you're picked off.

"You also get to come in for all those conferences on the mound," said John Kruk, the onetime blithe spirit of the Phillies. "I always liked listening in, though to tell you the truth, you never learned a whole lot."

It was at first base that another Phillie, Dick Allen, made his mark—in more ways than one.

Horrendously strong and enormously talented, Allen wielded a bat the size of a telephone pole. He clubbed 351 homers in his career, most of them caught by the man in the moon.

He eventually fell from favor among the Phillies fans, who perceived him to fall short of expectations—theirs, not his. So to while away his time, Allen took to using his cleats to scrawl messages in the dirt cutout around first. But these were not love letters in the sand. And to prove he had caught the Philadelphia spirit, he printed this:

Boo.

Catchers: Down and Dirty

MARCH 29, 2008

The door from the steam room opens, and Darren Daulton, leader of The Daulton Gang and of Macho Row, emerges, swathed in towels and fog, walking with the slow, deliberate gait of a sea captain feeling his way across a storm-tossed deck.

Daulton's knees make the sound of someone cracking walnuts. He sits heavily and says: "Takes a while to get all the parts back where they belong."

And so it does. Such is the life of a catcher, the toughest position in all of sports. And so it is on this midsummer night in 1993, with the game long over, with everyone else long gone, that only Daulton remains, trying to undo the damage that accumulates from all those knee-crippling frog squats in the dirt, on a steamy 90-degree night, encased in armor, scrambling to block pitches in the dirt, shaking off the foul tips that rip into you like shrapnel.

Yes, sir, a glamorous position this number two. Glamorous, indeed. That is, if you're partial to pain.

Daulton and his successor as catcher of the Phillies, Mike Lieberthal, went under the knife more than two dozen times in their careers, most of the cutting done on their knees, though nothing hurts quite like the foul tip on the meat hand. You can always tell the catcher—he's the one whose fingers point in different directions.

Once, a catcher's gear was described as the Tools of Ignorance. Only the ignorant would say that. For no one else in the game has as many responsibilities as position number two: the base runner who wants to test your arm, the one who wants to get you lined up in his crosshairs for one of those home-plate collisions, the umpire you try to sweet-talk to get the marginal pitch called in your favor . . . and, oh yes, the pitchers. Some you coax, some you cuss. Some you have to make brave. Some you have to soothe. Divas and prima donnas. Cy Young and Sigh Jung. Starters who lie about what they've got left and wild-eyed relievers with their exasperating 37-pitch half-innings. Sometimes, you feel like you ought to have a psychiatrist's couch strapped to your back.

And, of course, you're supposed to hit as well, a task most colorfully described by that eminent catcher and philosopher, Lawrence Peter "Yogi" Berra: "You can't think and hit at the same time."

Asked to select the best catcher of all time, the vote here would be cast in favor of Johnny Bench, the anchor of Cincinnati's Big Red Machine. His pitchers found his easy style of receiving comforting; they said it was like throwing to a man in a rocking chair. He also had 2,000 hits, 381 home runs and almost 1,400 RBI.

There are some who say the best catcher was a player very few people actually saw play. According to the records, Josh Gibson of the Homestead Grays of the Negro National League belted exactly 800 home runs. Few tried to steal and none tried to run him over. And pitchers learned quickly never to shake him off.

For sheer endurance, for pure down-home New England granite toughness, there has never been one the equal of Carlton Ernest Fisk, a.k.a. "Pudge." He is best known for the 1975 World Series when he struck what looked to be either a heroic home run or a tantalizing foul, the ball curving toward the left-field foul pole and Fisk waving at it frantically, willing the ball to stay fair.

Which it did.

Fisk always reminded me of a medieval knight, clanking along in his armor, jousting with dragons. No catcher ever logged more seasons (24), nor played more games (one shy of exactly 2,500). He walked away. On his own terms.

Which, when you think on it, is a triumph in itself.

Pitchers: Make the Ball
Sit Up and Speak

MARCH 30, 2008

There's a physicist, Dizzy Dean was once told, who says he can prove that the curveball is nothing more than an optical illusion. To which Dizzy replied: "You tell that scientist feller to stand behind that tree over yonder, and I'll whump him with an optical illusion."

Well, it can be made to curve, of course. Or drop. Or rise. Or sink. Or dance like a butterfly with the hiccups. It can, in the calloused hands of a seasoned fireballer, be delivered at supersonic speeds.

But at a fearsome cost.

For there is no more unnatural act in sports than pitching a baseball. It is a violent, traumatic, wrenching movement, a concussive insult to the wrist, elbow and shoulder. Over time, the toll includes bone fragments, shredded ligaments, eroded tendons and mysterious words like labrum and rotator cuff. And inevitably, Tommy John surgery.

And yet, be honest now, who among us has not fantasized as a position number one, perched imposingly on the mound, peering down with an imperious sneer while the catcher wig-wags signals and the batter, well aware of the high heat you can bring, twitches nervously and tries not to let his front foot bail out? Trade a lifetime of not being able to comb your hair for the chance to pitch in the bigs? Where do I sign?

How about being reincarnated as Nolan Ryan? Seven no-hitters. And maybe even more impressive, 12 one-hitters. Almost 6,000 strikeouts. Trying to hit him, Willie Stargell said, was like trying to eat soup with a fork.

You have two choices of pitching style: gas or guile. Flame or finesse. You can be the Ryan Express, a freak of nature still leaving a vapor trail in your 40s. Or you can nibble and frustrate, like, say, a Greg Maddux. Up and in. Low and away. Every direction except straight. A subtle change of speeds, five miles per hour here, 10 there, but always with the same exact arm speed.

The late Johnny Podres was especially fond of the change-up because, he said, with the change-up the batter does your work for you—lunging, off balance and overanxious, he tends to get himself out. And look foolish at the same time.

One of the most intriguing careers was that of Sandy Koufax, who needed six seasons before he could finally harness his control. And then, for a five-year stretch, he was literally untouchable—four no-hitters in four back-to-back seasons, a two-year combined total in 1965-66 of 54 wins, 668 innings pitched and 679 strikeouts.

This was when the game was played in a simpler time, before pitch counts and all sorts of set-up specialists and relievers. Koufax retired abruptly. His left elbow was permanently bent. He had traumatic arthritis. He could barely lift his arm. He had paid the price.

When the Phillies won the 1980 World Series, their Irish leprechaun, the reliever Tug McGraw, had pitched and pitched and pitched, yet kept taking the ball.

Don't you have a sore arm?

"You better believe it."

What do you do for it?

"Tape aspirin to my elbow."

Sometimes, it's really a simple game.

The Fans: A Pew in the
Church of Baseball

MARCH 31, 2008

Of all the congregations who worship in the Church of Baseball, none have been as steadfast and true, as unflaggingly faithful, as forgiving of transgressions, as the penitents who pledge themselves—lock, stock and soul every spring—to the Phillies of Philadelphia.

If ever there has been an inexplicable triumph of heart over head, of passion over reason, this is it.

Oh, to be sure, for a time the camp followers of the Boston Red Sox could blather on and on about their luckless misery, delivering self-flagellating monologues about their suffering. Woe is us, woe is us. Now, of course, with two championships in this century alone, such indulgent posturing rings hollow.

Same for those who have found it chic to claim to be fans of the Cubs of Chicago. But in fact, compared to the Fightin's and their rooters, they are mere Johnny-come-latelies to this business of consistent, persistent losing.

No, the Phillies stand alone. Unequaled at being inept, they have compiled more losing seasons than anyone else, and subjected their followers to agony of biblical proportions. And still the people come.

In 125 years of attempting to commit baseball, they have won one championship. One. And still the people come. This season just past, they became the first team in any professional sport to rack up 10,000 defeats. And still the people come.

Upwards of 125 million—million!—have passed through the turnstiles. Who knows how many times that have followed the Phillies by car radio, by TV, by transistor, from bars, from recliners, from porches front and back?

This Trail of Tears has meandered through parts of three centuries, and still the people come. Ironic is their fealty because, like many Philadelphia fans, they can be acid-tongued, rashly judgmental and blindingly fatalistic.

And yet their loyalty to their baseball team is handed down, almost reverently, generation to generation to generation to generation. To be a Phillies fan is to hear what you want to hear and, sometimes, to see what you think you hear.

I submit this as proof: Some years ago, the late Bus Saidt, a sportswriter who chronicled the Phillies, was listening to their game on a car radio. It was close and tight, with the winning run on base when the umpire rang up strike three. Fightin's lose. Bus, apoplectic, leaned down until his chin was almost touching the radio and snarled: "That pitch was way outside. You are pathetic!"

In every pew in the Church of Baseball, they nod their understanding. When the game gets its hook into you, you are gaffed forever.

Of all our sports, baseball gives us the most to work with. It is awash in statistics, new numbers invented almost annually, and the game has become so filled with minutia that it is possible to decipher so much information from a box score that you can all but recreate each game, pitch by pitch.

And the game bridges past with present. At my grandfather's knee, I learned about baseball. We would sit in the shade and listen to whatever game was on the radio, and he would draw up his own box score and then, with the stub of a pencil, with loving care, he would enter the numbers. He might as well have preserved them in amber.

Baseball is rife with rituals, and each game is played to a sedate, familiar rhythm. Football captivates because it is played on a visceral level and satisfies the recommended daily allowance of what the American appetite craves—speed, collisions and blood. The formula is simple but brilliant: Mass times speed equals dents in your fender.

But the pace of baseball is more measured. There is a pitch-pause-pitch tempo. The game is meant for savoring, not inhaling. That is probably why it is such a hard sell to the young of today, who are busily occupied with surfing the Internet in search of porn to download.

Baseball has nature on its side. The season begins when the calendar has flipped over to the time of rebirth and renewal, when all things are fresh and new and burgeoning with promise, when nothing seems beyond our reach. In the spring, hope springs.

Even for Phillies fans.

Especially for Phillies fans.

3

Etc . . . Etc . . . Etc . . .

Missy: The Grin Lives On

DECEMBER 19, 1999

She could grin. Really, she could. People didn't believe it until they saw her do it.

You would grin at her and she would grin back: a big, sweeping, arcing, delirious up-swoosh of a grin. And the more you grinned at her, the more she grinned back, until there you were, a whole circle of grinning fools.

And you know what? When you're grinning, you can't do certain things. Like scream and shout. Or curse and damn. Or start an argument. Or say mean, spiteful, unkind things that you wish you could take back the moment they escape from your mouth.

When your face is split by a grin, then your whole body is locked in joy. Which is, when you think about it, not a bad way to go through life.

Which is what she understood. Which is what all dogs seem to understand.

We lost her last week. To cancer.

A more congenial companion you cannot imagine . . . well, unless you have a dog of your own. Then, you know.

Dogs touch the deepest part of us. There is a connection of souls. We find in them a kindred spirit, an understanding that needs no words.

For almost 11 years she was there to protect us and mother us and shepherd us. She was there without complaint or demand, without malice or deceit, patient and enduring beyond all reason, grateful just to be acknowledged, offering unconditional and totally selfless love.

She was small but mighty. And feisty. She thought she was bigger than she was. The blood of her ancestor, the wolf, may have been diluted by the years, but it still coursed through her.

On two legs, she would have been a point guard. Or a second baseman. Or a cornerback. Coaches would have loved her attitude. And her grit and her pluck.

She was a sprinter of impressive acceleration, and she had a vertical leap to astonish you—from a sitting position, she could leap almost twice her own height up onto the bed. She was always surprised that you were surprised by this. And when you made such a big deal out of it, you could swear she actually blushed.

We would lie on that bed and watch the late-night games together, eating ice cream straight from the tub—a spoon for you, a spoon for me. Neither one of us ever had the sense to know when to stop.

And if this strikes you as excessive doting, you are referred to an old saying: If you think a dog should be treated like a dog, then you probably shouldn't have a dog.

She was the better judge of competitive worth in a sporting contest. She could sense a blowout coming and was usually asleep before you, and when you reached for the remote in disgust, she would look at you as if to say: Finally wised up, huh? I could have told you that game was going to be a turkey.

She was three months old when we got her. She was a fast study. In almost no time at all she had us trained.

What other creatures can understand exactly what you're saying even though they themselves are forever without the power of speech? What other creatures can communicate to you precisely what they want simply by the canine pantomime of certain, specific ears-up, tail-signaling looks that you come to recognize?

It is why you can imagine dogs comparing owners, one saying to the other: "He's a little slow, but I've worked with him and I think, all in all, you know, considering his obvious limitations, that he's come along nicely."

Our lady had a piercing bark, and she was a zealous defender of her turf, and she was more than tolerant when it came to the illogic of what we expected from her: Be a good, alert watchdog, and when she would dutifully obey that directive and raise a fine ruckus at the first footfall of a stranger, then we would shush at her to shut up.

Don't you sometimes imagine that they must think to themselves: Well, make up your mind, which is it you want?

We suffered a power outage last summer. No electricity for three days and nights. As twilight approached, she would look at me expectantly, and then as darkness was enveloping us, she would look at her sister and you could swear they were telling each other: "Do you suppose it will ever dawn on this doofus to just turn on the light switch? If only we had thumbs."

Dogs have the rare gift of understanding that just sitting on grass and watching the world go by is not at all boring. Rather, it is peace. It is tranquility. It is a state to be earnestly desired.

We had come to think of our lady as indestructible. Through a terrible, unforgivable lapse on her human's part, she had had both her front paws run over by a car. To the absolute amazement of the veterinarian, the X-rays showed not a single fractured bone.

He made the sign of the cross to bless her and said: "Missy, you redefine what 'lucky dog' means."

In no time, she was back accelerating from zero to 60.

Another time, one of her fang-teeth was ripped almost out. It hung at a 90-degree angle. The vet repositioned it, made a mighty shove, and jammed it back in place. The medical manuals, he said, claim that it is sometimes possible for the tooth to reattach. Sure enough, it worked. Lucky dog, indeed.

And then came the day when she began to slow. Soon, she was content to merely watch the squirrels she used to chase. She seemed to age overnight.

Her legs betrayed her. She suffered the indignity of incontinence. She quit eating.

The tumors were everywhere inside her. Chemotherapy might give her a few weeks, they said, but she would be constantly sick and suffering.

So we did what you do in such agonizing circumstances. We cried until we had no more tears, and then we cried some more, and then we presumed to bestow upon her the release of euthanasia, praying that it is right to extinguish the light under such conditions, and asking her forgiveness for our arrogance.

The lasting memory will be of that glorious white plume of a tail that would shoot up like a periscope and set to wagging madly the instant she heard your voice. Was anyone ever as happy to see you, and never mind that you had only been gone for 15 minutes?

Her legacy will be The Grin . . . and the remembrance that when your face is occupied by a grin, it has no room for scowl or frown or snarl.

And you have no room for an unkind thought, or the heart to give voice to it.

Blue Rocks:
A Generation Bridged

JULY 22, 2003

The grass is never quite as impossibly green, the echo-chamber thwack-thwack-thwack of bat on ball never quite as sharp, the air never quite as thick with anticipation and possibility, as when you are seven years old and finding your seat for a professional baseball game.

"Pop-Pop, look, these are very good seats," Joshua says, locked in awe, Christmas morning wide of eye, heart working like a bunny rabbit's twitching nose.

"Yes. Yes, they are," Pop-Pop agrees, pleased with the proximity to the field and with the unobstructed sight lines.

"Because," Joshua says, "see, the snack bar is right over there."

Pop-Pop sights along the small finger that, like a quivering spaniel on point, is fixed on the refreshment stand, which is, indeed, no more than 20 paces distant. Then Pop-Pop's eye scans to the right and lands on another sign, one that is as welcome as rain in a drought:

"Men's room."

Pop-Pop is almost as ecstatic over this discovery as Joshua is about the snack bar.

For this, you see, is the inevitable, unavoidable and universal difference in generations, two of the stages in the life cycle of man: When we are seven, nothing seems nearly so seductive as candy. And when we are 65, ahhhh, nothing feels quite so welcome and reassuring as an oasis for bladder relief.

At Daniel S. Frawley Stadium in Wilmington, the clean, well-appointed and bust-a-gut-trying, consumer-friendly home of the Wilmington Blue Rocks of the Carolina League, just off I-95, neither snack bars nor water closets are ever very far away. From time to time, when the arrogance and avarice of SportsWorld feel like a tightening noose, it can be restorative to retreat, to return to roots. And in the summer, minor-league baseball is to be highly recommended as a refresher.

On this night, members of the Rattlers, a team that has concluded its season in the Mickey Vernon Little League, have come as a group, in chattering cacophony and squirming with bounding, boundless energy. The next time a sour mood tries to coil its depressing bleakness around you, spend a soft summer night in the company of a giggling gaggle of seven-

and eight- and nine-year-olds at a minor-league baseball game. The blues
will evaporate like dew at dawn.

On this night, a ticket is seven dollars; group rate, a buck off. The seat
is but 13 rows from the field, just to the left of home plate. Parking is—
brace yourself—free. For all. So are the Blue Rocks baseball caps, part of
a giveaway night. The ticket-takers thank you for coming. They smile. Such
a concept.

The players sign autographs almost up to the first pitch.

And here is the absolute best part of all: As each Blue Rock is introduced and trots to his position, a child is assigned to him and accompa-
nies him onto the playing field, and stays with him, cap off and over the
heart, during the National Anthem. Then the children scurry away and you
are willing to wager that their feet never really touch the ground.

Like most strokes of marketing genius, this one is so simple as to leave
you asking: Why don't the Big Boys do this? Why, for that matter, doesn't
everyone do this?

You have created, on the spot, a memory for a lifetime.

More, you have created a fan for a lifetime, someone devoted not only
to your team but to your sport.

The little ones scamper off the field and play commences. In the first
few innings, the foul balls fall like hailstones, and the Rattlers, who have
come equipped with their gloves, pop up and down out of their seats with
such eager alacrity that soon you come to feel as if you are in a prairie dog
village.

The opponents, the Lynchburg (Virginia) Hillcats, score two runs in
the first when their designated hitter, Chris Shelton, who at that moment
is leading the Carolina League in both batting average (.352) and home
runs (17), crushes a 400-foot shot to left-center.

The Rattlers boo.

The Blue Rocks respond with three runs in their half of the first. Each
time the home team scores, a person dressed as a stalk of celery, one of
several of the team's zany mascots, comes out and dances about in frantic, joyous and dizzying circles. Very soon the Rattlers learn to chant, in
earnest and high-pitched fervor: "We want the celery. We want the celery."

Surely it will be the only time in their entire lives that they will clamor
so passionately for a vegetable.

The between-innings gimmicks and games unfurl in an endless, beat-
the-boredom rhythm. Baby Race. Sombrero Catch. Daddy Dash. Plunger
Toss. A scrum involving a giant peanut, a giant hot dog and a giant bag of
popcorn. A sing-along to the theme song from SpongeBob SquarePants,
whose rollicking lyrics are contained in the title.

In the bottom of the seventh, the ritual singing of "Take Me Out to the Ball Game" is loud and lusty and heartfelt. And "I don't care if I never get back" sounds especially sincere.

The visitors' slugger, Shelton, clubs another mammoth homer in the eighth to tie it at 3-3. But the Blue Rocks scratch out a run in their half of the eighth when their catcher, Tony Arnerich, is plunked by a pitch with the bases loaded. It is the essence of taking one for the team.

The Blue Rocks hold in the ninth. Everyone leaves happy.

It occurs to you that "minor league" is a grievous misnomer. There is nothing at all minor here.

"Maybe we could come back, huh, Pop-Pop?" Joshua asks.

Pop-Pop, stricken by the emotional, circle-of-life quality of this night, develops a sudden catch in his throat and nods, and when he regains his voice, he says: "We could stop by the snack bar on the way out, if you want."

Joshua considers this and thoughtfully says: "Yes, and the men's room, too."

Miss Kimbee:
The View from the Rear

AUGUST 21, 1988

Wilmington.

The introductions are made in the barn. The female is three years old, just over six feet tall, not counting the tips of her pointy ears. Having just polished off a hearty breakfast, she goes 1200 pounds. She is the color of dark copper. She can be claimed for $4,000.

The male is 50, six feet four, 198 pounds. He is, owing to a condition known as abject fear, the color of chalk. He can be had, as his wife is relentlessly fond of pointing out, for considerably less than $4,000.

The female, her shoes making clopping sounds on the stall floor, steps forward daintily. She is curious. The male, his knees making sounds like castanets, steps backward, lurching. He is petrified.

"The idea," Marv Bachrad of Brandywine Raceway, and as of that moment a former friend, is explaining, "is a celebrity drivers race. Miss Kimbee will be your horse."

Miss Kimbee tries to be polite, but clearly she is less than thrilled with the prospect of being chauffeured by the rankest sort of amateur. Worse, a novice. An absolute beginner. A total innocent. A Pilgrim.

It was considered prudent to be introduced before the actual race, to even take a get-acquainted jog, especially since The Pilgrim had never so much as brushed up against a sulky.

Miss Kimbee is trained and normally driven by Larry MacDonald, an experienced horseman and the most agreeable of men. That he was willing to entrust a member of his stable to such an endeavor spoke volumes about his generosity. Either that, or whatever Marv Bachrad has got on him includes pictures.

The Pilgrim is instructed in how to sit in the bike. The Pilgrim is instructed in how to hold the reins. (Pretend you're holding a bird: too tight, and you squeeze him to death; too loose, and he flies away.)

The Pilgrim gets cocky. He almost has an accident on the way from the barn to the jogging track. There is a parked car. Miss Kimbee walks determinedly toward it.

Maybe five feet before she will bump into it, Larry MacDonald, without a trace of panic, almost nonchalantly tells The Pilgrim: "You know, if you don't pull on the reins to let her know she's supposed to turn, she'll just keep on going. They're totally dependent on the driver to steer them."

It's not rocket science. Even The Pilgrim understands the basics. Pull on the left rein, they go left. Pull right, they go right. Pull on both and they stop.

You hope.

"One thing more," says Larry MacDonald. "Sometimes she'll stumble. She loses concentration."

Swell.

Miss Kimbee knows the routine. The morning jog is as familiar to a racehorse as roadwork at dawn to a boxer, or hamstring-stretching to a sprinter. She falls into an easy, half-speed gait. Nothing too taxing but enough to break a sweat. She snorts, clearing her sinuses. Four miles. Eight times around the track. And, oh yes, watch out for the water truck.

The Pilgrim is struck most by the obvious power. You can feel it through the lines, in the clip-clopping ease. Power. Horsepower. Except there is no hood covering up this engine.

Which brings us to another point. The view from the bike is not the most glamorous. It's not sunset on Maui. It's not Center City Philadelphia spread before you at the top of the Art Museum steps.

There are two hindquarters, like the pistons on a locomotive, and the first fearful thought is that one, or both, is going to deliver to you a kick square in the chops. This is, of course, an optical illusion, brought on by terror. There is also a twitching tail. And—there's just no diplomatic way around this—the south end of a horse going north.

But the view quickly becomes secondary to the sensation of all that power. Visualize half a dozen men, each a robust 200-pounder, pulling you along with contemptuous ease.

Larry MacDonald, jogging another horse, pulls up alongside. "Chirp to her," he says, grinning.

The Pilgrim manages to work up enough saliva to click his tongue against the roof of his mouth. It is weak, but it registers with Miss Kimbee. She shifts to another gear. The acceleration reminds you of teenage drag duels on Saturday night.

In a race, with all that noise, the drumbeat of hooves, the creaking of equipment, drivers yelling, making a chirp would be about as effectual as whistling in the midst of an air raid.

The best drivers have the hands of concert pianists. Or safecrackers. They communicate through the reins.

"The good ones," Marv Bachrad says, "make a horse feel brave. They'll always hold back a little so the horse feels like it can still go faster, like it's got a lot left."

Some drivers use the whip. For noise, mostly, smacking the shaft, the wheels. Others will play with the reins, fluttering them. And some sing.

One driver's trademark is to sing hymns to his horse all the way around the track, not to save his soul but to hoard his speed, and if he has timed it right, at the top of the stretch he will bellow out, "Ama-a-a-zing gra-a-a-ace, how sweet the sounnnd," and the horse, divinely inspired, will cut loose and thunder home.

There is one driver who sings to his horses in Hungarian.

Miss Kimbee will be spared such motivation. The Pilgrim is tone-deaf. Besides, his ambitions are modest. His most burning desire is that he, the horse and the sulky arrive at the finish line simultaneously. Intact. With the tires rubber-side up.

The morning of the race, The Pilgrim jogs another horse. On Brandy-wine's main track. Behind the starter car.

This horse, Precious Skip, has just won his last race. Impressively. There are high hopes for him. He is good and he knows it.

Still, for a hotshot, he seems sluggish.

During the course of this workout, just about the time The Pilgrim is convinced the harness-driving business is a snap, Precious Skip answers nature's call.

Once. Twice. A third time.

This is most definitely not Maui at sunset.

The Pilgrim's eyes begin to water.

"One of the reasons we jog them every morning is for just that, to clean 'em out," says Jim Doherty Jr., the trainer and driver. "It's the sign of a healthy horse."

This has to be the healthiest horse on the premises.

Plus, Precious Skip has chosen this morning to have enough gas to light up several municipalities.

Jim, about those baked–bean breakfasts. . . . It's not as though you can bail out on a bike.

"Welcome to show business," says Marv Bachrad cheerfully.

Race night.

One mile. Once and a half around the Brandywine track, which is hard and swift. Field of five.

Miss Kimbee, three-year-old bay filly, by Brand New Fella and out of Miss Siladios, is making her 26th career start. With her largest handicap ever: the driver.

Call to the post parade.

Final instructions.

"Best not to go to the lead with her," Larry MacDonald advises. "Tuck in behind someone along the rail and sit there. Get to the stretch and then you can turn her loose."

The Pilgrim nods his understanding.

So, of course, Miss Kimbee goes right to the lead.

She is smoking.

It isn't The Pilgrim's idea. He is just along for the ride.

Miss Kimbee is full of race. During the post parade she is rammy, ready, barely controllable.

She will not be held back. The math is simple: 200 pounds doesn't dictate to 1200 pounds.

Miss Kimbee races her guts out.

She gets the lead and holds it. All the way until the final five yards before the finish line.

When they have found their best stride, pacers roll from side to side, like ships in heavy, heaving seas. Miss Kimbee is rolling, surging, but the pace is ill-advised. The first half-mile is gone in one minute, two seconds.

A killer pace. A foolish pace. Driver error.

The Pilgrim takes too long to get Miss Kimbee over to the rail. For much of the race, they take the long way around the track. The Pilgrim will berate himself for this later.

If you had saved ground with her earlier, he will scold himself over and over, she might have had enough left in the stretch.

But she doesn't.

Rounding the last turn, The Pilgrim knows they're coming. First you feel it. The ground shakes. Then you hear it. Thunderclaps. Hoofbeats. Hard and fast.

The Pilgrim chirps madly. He flops the lines desperately. He wishes he knew Hungarian. He wishes he could get out and run for her.

Miss Kimbee is an athlete and she is trying. Lord, how she is trying. But now she is coming apart. Her breathing is forced, her gait floundering.

The Pilgrim is filled with urgency. And also with a pride and a love for the way she is trying—for her courage, her gallantry. He tries to will her to hold together.

But they are coming, on the outside, two of them. The finish line is in view. The Pilgrim tries to wish it closer.

But no. At the wire, two horses flash by, a blur.

Miss Kimbee is third. She deserves better. She deserves a better driver.

"When this is over," Bachrad had told The Pilgrim, "you'll feel such a rush, you'll feel so exhilarated, you'll want to do it again."

He is, it turns out, absolutely correct.

The Pilgrim, on an incredible adrenalin high, wants another go. Right now.

Miss Kimbee, panting, indicates that she'd appreciate the chance to catch her breath first.

9/11 I:
Never a Surrender

SEPTEMBER 16, 2001

And so, here in September, while we kneel and remember, the sound of silence is upon our playgrounds.

Our stadiums sit empty as ghost towns. Our ballparks are as quiet as churches.

There are no crowd roars, no guttural rise of anticipation, no low-throated moan of despair. No one gathers around the tribal campfires of the tailgaters.

Bat and ball do not meet. Linebacker and running back do not collide.

Our TV screens flicker not with images of touchdowns scored or home runs struck or cheerleaders catapulted to the clouds, but of helmets removed, caps placed over hearts, heads bowed.

This is customarily our safe harbor—sports. This is our refuge—sports. This is where we come to lose ourselves—here in sports.

But not this weekend.

For now, there is a moratorium. For now, we stand respectfully aside, as we should. For now, there is solemnity, grief, mourning and remembrance. Plenty of time to get back to the playing fields.

We bury the known dead while the searchers dig grimly on and relatives cling to the hope that the missing somehow have found a pocket inside that awful rubble, a protective cocoon, and wait to be found.

How unseemly it would have been to be playing today. How disrespectful, how insensitive, how inappropriate.

Some argued that we should have played on, that diversion and distraction would have been healthy, that by allowing unspeakable tragedy to make us pause, we did precisely what our evil attackers wanted us to, that they succeeded because we capitulated.

There is no right or wrong answer to such a conundrum. It is like religion; it is what you happen to believe.

But while sports offers an escape from reality, there is some reality that should not be cast off quite so casually.

This thought cannot be shaken: If you were burying someone today, would games matter to you at all?

Besides, this was only a timeout. It was never a surrender.

Tomorrow, we begin again.

Tomorrow, the world comes back to us, and it will matter again, though certainly not as much as before, whether Barry Bonds can club eight more home runs, whether Michael Jordan is parachuting back into the game yet again.

Tomorrow, it will matter again that the Eagles have a game plan, and it is not for Tampa Bay now but for Seattle.

Tomorrow night, it will matter again that the Phillies, themselves survivors of a different sort, are still pursuing a pennant, and that the Braves, from whom they must seize it, are in town for four games, and that these are terribly important games. And yet, in light of all that has befallen America in six days, maybe not quite as terribly important as we thought a week ago.

All things are relative, none more so than when you are at war.

Major League Baseball has added a week to its season, and a corresponding week to its playoffs. The World Series creeps to the brink of November.

The National Football League has discarded one of its 16 Sundays, and there will not be an easy way to reclaim it.

The NFL had no choice. Literally. Its players—almost to a man on some teams—did not want to play, and said so. They went further than that. Some of them had said they would not play even if ordered to do so, regardless of the consequences.

Such was the strength and the depth of their convictions. And, frankly, of their fears. They did not want to rush onto a plane. They did not want to present themselves as unprotected targets in an open arena, ringed by tens of thousands of equally unprotected targets.

Who can blame them?

What would the NFL have done in the face of such a mutiny, or wildcat strike?

The embarrassment would have been much greater than that which accrued from the lamentable and lamented decision to play days after the assassination of President John F. Kennedy.

But they, and we, have been spared.

The belief here is that the right thing was done.

As our referees and our umpires are forever reminding us, getting it right is the prevailing aim, and if you happen to need instant replay or a peer's input, that is OK, as long as you get it right.

So we near the end of our timeout. The games begin again soon. Sports has always been about rallying, about the getting back up rather than the getting knocked down.

Athletes are forever telling you how they did what they could.

You were reminded of that while watching on television a man being interviewed as he reclined on a donor table, a tube siphoning off a pint of his best type O, which he had volunteered for a reason that made you blink back tears as you listened to him: "This is all I can do, so I'm doing it."

Amen. Amen. Amen.

9/11 II:
Remember September

SEPTEMBER 5, 2002

The NFL season was two days old. The Eagles had lost their opener, had lost it at home, had lost a game they should have won against the St. Louis Rams, had lost it in overtime, had lost it by a field goal.

And now, still kicking themselves over such a squandered opportunity, the Birds were regrouping to play at Tampa Bay.

They would, eventually. But not until January.

Because The Unspeakable intervened.

And now, the first anniversary of The Unspeakable rushes toward us, and it comes at us like the mournful, seductive call of a freight train in the night, or the heart-stabbing melancholy of a lone bagpiper somewhere in the mist, squeezing out the haunting strains of "Amazing Grace."

Six days till 9/11.

One year later, we are left with a hole in Manhattan and a hole in our heart.

Grief is like religion, a thing to be done with the heart and on one's own terms, none of it anybody else's business.

Sports generally acquitted itself well immediately after The Unspeakable. Baseball suspended play. The NFL took the week off. There was a moratorium on almost all games, all sports, as was only right and proper.

A few argued that to cease for a moment would be to give in to the terrorists, that the distraction of sport would be a welcome palliative. But this was much, much too overwhelming. This was The Unspeakable, and to not pause would have been to trivialize the tragedy.

The first anniversary of The Unspeakable falls in midweek. So whatever observances football has in mind will have to be this weekend. Baseball has announced it will mark the anniversary with video tributes, a moment of silence during games, and a commemorative message on the bases and balls.

We need the release and the remembrance. We need the silent moment. And perhaps the trumpet's tearful "Taps."

We need the pause for perspective, for the reassurance of priorities, the nudging, forceful elbow that reminds us of sports' proper place.

We need the prayer for peace, the one for thanksgiving, and the one for understanding.

And the one for celebration, too—the one that says we survive, we endure, we shall overcome.

The return to play last September was done in a tone of impassioned defiance, the message to the terrorists a thunderous, ringing shout of resistance: "Yo! We're still here. You did your worst, now we'll do our best."

The flags were the size of football fields, unfurled by firemen and policemen and athletes, the latter being reminded of their proper place in the grand scheme, and of who the real heroes are.

In the year since, some of the pledges that were made have been kept and just as many not. Some of the vows have been honored and quite a few not. We promised to do certain things in a certain way, as we tend to do when scared. We promised to reform our ways.

Maybe we have, but there has been backsliding, too. As there always, inevitably is. As there always, inevitably will be, if for no reason more complicated than this: the inhabitants of the third rock from the sun are, in every weak and strong, every timid and triumphant way, most assuredly human.

And so, as in our sports, we persist, following that old mantra of the locker room: Give it your best shot.

In the year since The Unspeakable, tears have dried, and yet can be summoned by no more than a picture, a fragment of a thought.

The soldiers with the guns have left the airports. At some arenas, we have to park farther away, which is, really, a small inconvenience, though from listening to us, you'd think it an enormous sacrifice.

Those of us who chronicle the games must submit our bags and computers for search, though this has deteriorated into a haphazard, half-hearted, wave-'em-on-through exercise.

Some say our privacy has been violated, and so the terrorists have somehow won, and we edge ever closer to the reign of Big Brother.

But the enduring image of 9/11 that I have is from a hot June day out on Long Island, at a golf course named Bethpage Black, site of the U.S. Open, and about 50 miles from Ground Zero. A fireman named John Caputo has presented a golf ball to the United States Golf Association.

Not just any golf ball.

This one was on the 20th floor in the South Tower of the World Trade Center the morning of The Unspeakable. A building, a colossus of a building, fell on it, and yet there it was, seven months later, virtually unmarked, without a crease or dent or cut.

Caputo had been raking through the debris of Ground Zero in April when a flash of white caught his eye. At first, he assumed it was a bone.

But no, it was a golf ball, dust-streaked, but otherwise without a trace of anything to suggest what it had endured.

The people crowded around it that day at the Open and stared at it in hushed reverence, as though it were a religious object. People blinked away tears and smiled at each other.

For the symbolism was unmistakable. A golf ball of all things, this little golf ball, had absorbed a titanic blow and, except for streaks of dust, was still there, intact. It endured.

As have we.

Atlanta Bombing:
Triumph Out of Tragedy

JULY 28, 1996

His name is Matt Ghaffari and he is a great bear of a man who wrestles for the United States, loses the gold medal match to a Russian titan, and then on the victory platform begins to cry uncontrollably, his huge body shaking with sobs.

And his father, who fled Iran 19 years ago to come to the United States and make a new life possible, hurries to his son and they embrace, and then Matt Ghaffari draws away and with great care removes the silver medal from around his thick neck and places it around his father's.

"For you, Papa," he says.

And the father cradles his son's round face in both his hands and the tears start down his face, and he says: "Oh my boy...my boy...."

I wept at that moment, and the memory of it makes me mist up still.

For that is the special gift of the Olympics, the gift of emotional release.

The best part of the Olympics always has been that it is a therapeutic, 2$^1/_2$–week emotional binge that allows us to clean out our tear ducts and fill our hearts.

Just about the time we have given up on humankind, along come the Olympics to replenish our soul and restore our spirit.

And so the Olympics always have been The Crying Games.

Today, sadly, they are even more so.

Yet a wonderful thing occurred yesterday, after a bomb exploded in the Centennial Olympic Park downtown. The Games went on anyway. For of all the terrible damage the flying shrapnel and the nails did, the one thing they could not touch was the essence of the human spirit.

So rowers rowed and then bent over their oars in exhaustion. And sprinters ran holes through the wind. And volleyball players hit thunderous spikes and made skittering saves. And not a single athlete asked to be excused, and as the President observed, their courage makes the cowardice of the bombers even more shameful.

And the people kept coming, no small act of bravery in itself, and an act of defiance, too. To stay away is to be held hostage. To stay away is to yield and to encourage the psychotic.

Play on? By all means.
Mourn? Definitely.
Surrender? Never.
It goes to the very soul of the Olympics.

His name is Victor Sinyak, and he is a 130–pound weightlifter from
Belarus, and he is down to his very last chance in the competition. In the
corridor, he leans against a wall in fatigue and his coach is grabbing him
and shaking him, and now he is slapping Sinyak's cheeks, hard and sting-
ing, and the coach is shouting, the veins popping out, and his tired athlete slowly begins to respond. It is emotional CPR.

And Victor Sinyak rouses himself for one last try, goes out and bends
over and grasps the bar and gives it a mighty, mighty tug, and the weight
rises slowly…and then it stops. Victor Sinyak has nothing left. The weights
crash to the floor and the lifter slumps away, sagging in disgrace.

His coach is waiting for him at the bottom of the steps, his face no
longer stern now but soft with compassion, and he is enfolding his athlete
in a tender embrace. Victor Sinyak is crying into his coach's shoulder, and
the coach is whispering in his athlete's ear.

"He is telling him," the interpreter says, "that he loves him."

When you least expect it, people are capable of stunning deeds.

Yes, these Games have been awash in transportation problems. Yes,
they are tacky. Yes, they are unpardonably commercial. But these are, in
the grander scheme, really nothing more than minor annoyances, made
even more inconsequential now by a random act of unconscionable violence.

But all the good stuff, ah, that is still here. The stuff that matters.

The best part of the Games is, well, the games. And the people who
play them—who play with valor and resiliency, who play in pain and
through exhaustion, who play with grit that never fails to astound you.
And then they cry in defeat and cry in triumph and cry leaning against
one another, and in the process set the rest of us to weeping, too.

I am of Irish heritage and accordingly I cry over sunsets, and I con-
fess that the highlight of my Olympics occurred when a $2^1/_2$–year–old
voice told me over the phone from 800 miles away: "Wuv ooo, Pop–Pop."
It turned me into a puddle.

So I am easy meat for television, which manipulates our emotions so
cleverly, so shamelessly, anyway. But more and more while our other sports
deteriorate, undone by avarice and arrogance, I find salvation in the
Olympics. And there was an extra helping of it yesterday.

Her name is Angel Martino and she is an American swimmer, and no sooner is a medal put around her neck than she takes it off and hands it to a woman of about 20 named Trisha Henry, whom Martino came to know at a swim camp run by Angel's father. Trisha Henry is fighting cancer.

"You have inspired me all this summer," Martino told the stricken woman. "I hope this doesn't embarrass you, but you are my hero."

We will not be intimidated, the President said yesterday. And so the people came. The looked determined, not cowed. If anything, their spirit for the Olympics seemed heightened.

It is possible at any venue to look up from live competition and see a series of television screens on which Dominique Moceanu, 72–pound gymnast, flies about like Tinkerbell, and to her right a 300–pound wrestler, Alexander Karelin, is grappling with a man the approximate size of a condo.

On one screen there may be a shell, sleek as a torpedo, slicing through the water, the rowers in synchronized grunting, and on the screen next to it a man badly in need of electrolysis all over his body whirls round and round and then releases a hammer.

It is all around at the Games, contrast like this, contrast and endless variety. They run like cheetahs, turn a pool to churning froth, leap up and seem never to come back down. And more times than not, they will do something, say something, that will make you dab at your eyes.

We yearn for heroes. We ache for something to make us root.

So a child woman of 80 pounds named Kerri Strug scurries down the runway on a leg aflame with pain and sticks a vault and wins the first team gold medal in the history of American women's gymnastics, and then must be carried on the victory platform. Well, even Machiavellian TV couldn't conjure up such theater.

When an American pair just misses qualifying for the finals in rowing and one of them crosses the finish line unconscious, having literally given his all, then Adam Holland says of his mate, Mike Peterson, the most lyrical thing I have heard one athlete say of another: "Someone gave me everything he had today and more, and if I'm ever lacking in inspiration I'll look back at this race and realize that someone gave me the ultimate gift."

In the name of such unquenchable spirit as that, the Olympics go on.

Barry Bonds:
A Joyless Pursuit

AUGUST 12, 2007

At nine minutes to midnight in the East, on Tuesday, August 7, in a major-league baseball park with all the splendor of San Francisco, its home, a bloated, gimpy-legged slugger works the pitch count to 3-and-2 and then turns on a fastball with a pristine, measured, disciplined stroke, and drives it well beyond the field of play, 435 feet being the consensus estimate.

And with that thunderclap, Barry Lamar Bonds, 43 years old and looking it, who has an ego to match his extravagant talent, a confounding contradiction of incandescent skills and surly temperament, became the most prolific producer of home runs in big-league history.

Not all were thrilled.

Thus endeth The Long March, an inch-by-agonizing-inch odyssey that commandeered the media and that served as more than passing distraction, impassioned debate and disillusionment.

The relief, as the ball settled into the grasping wolf pack of souvenir hunters in the right center–field bleachers, was palpable, like a roaring belch freeing you from the suffocation of indigestion.

Finally, thankfully, it was over. Let us resume life; let us get on with the matters at hand.

Usually, when an athlete pursues history, there is a sense of celebration, elation, anticipation. But Barry Bonds' stalking of Hank Aaron was pockmarked with frustration, denigration, vituperation.

In most venues beyond the City by the Bay, where Bonds has been accorded unconditional public love for at least the last five seasons, there is doubt and suspicion. He may be in the record books, but the spreading stain of steroid abuse will serve to blot it out.

Frankly, I am unsure what to feel exactly. Yes, the indicators point to guilt. At every turn. Yet, as Bonds himself has insisted, steroids did not sharpen his hand-eye coordination, did not improve his incredible selectivity and patience at the plate.

The great pity is what he could have been, even without pharmaceutical assistance. Barry Bonds was good. Wicked good. Hall of Fame good. Does the greatest home–run hitter in history belong in the Hall of Fame?

The sacred Hall is, after all, home of greatness, but also of shameful conduct: homer hitters and adulterers, 300–game winners and drunks.

I have always thought Pete Rose should be admitted to the Hall, with the proviso that his plaque list not only the unsurpassed 4,256 hits and all the other gaudy numbers, but also his transgressions, including betting on baseball and lying about it.

Same for Bonds.

I was in Atlanta for this paper 33 springs ago, chronicling Hank Aaron's dogged, dignified pursuit of Babe Ruth. I can still see Aaron, lean and lithe, six feet and 180 pounds, ironically the same size as the pre-steroids Bonds. I can still see Aaron's buggy-whip wrists snapping, and the ball burning through the night, into the left-field bullpen, caught by a relief pitcher named Tom House.

You've seen all the replays since, a million times, Aaron touring the bases with that same economy of emotion, scrupulously avoiding the celebration-of-me histrionics of today's athletes, and those two long-haired civilians (for the record, their names were Britt Gaston and Cliff Courtney), self-appointed escorts trotting between second and third.

The emotions I recall were awe and admiration, and they were a distinct contrast to the gastric-bubble-puncturing of number 756.

Perhaps no other player besides Jackie Robinson endured what Henry Aaron did as he closed in on Babe Ruth's record. The pressures were unimaginable, the threats of great harm very real. Yet he conducted himself with remarkable grace and aplomb.

He won over many, first by his class, later as a sort of elder statesman for the game. If you wanted to know his opinions, you had to ask; he was never one to shoot from the hip, or lip.

So when he steadfastly refused to be at the scene when Bonds surpassed him, he did provide a videotape of salute. But the fact that he was not there, and said he never would be, spoke volumes.

So what do we do? Well, what some see as a solution, or savior, appears to be in the wings, if not the on-deck circle. His name is Alex Rodriguez. The same week that Bonds caught Aaron, the man known as A-Rod became the youngest player ever to reach 500 home runs.

He is 32, and currently in the employ of the New York Yankees, perhaps the only franchise that can still afford him. Assume good health and assume that over, say, eight seasons, he averages 40 home runs a year—hardly an unrealistic expectation—that puts him at 820.

And he leaves Barry Bonds a disappearing dot in the rearview mirror.

A Gathering of Legends

OCTOBER 23, 1982

Atlantic City—Some of them are still flashy, and some of them are merely fleshy. Some of them have found a way to stop the aging process, and some of them wear the scars of dissipation with obvious pain.

Some of them still trade on their names—hucksters and shills for whatever doodads need selling on TV. The pancake makeup masks the years, and then they give their endorsements. It's a way to hang onto the spotlight a little while longer, and, hey, the royalty checks never hurt, either.

And some of them have found letting go wasn't all that difficult, that there is, indeed, life after sports. And although they have faded from memory and have become lines in the record book and answers to trivia questions, they have their memories to warm them in the winters.

A lot of them have gathered here this weekend, tanned and breezy and confident, playing golf and telling harmless exaggerations—some of them bemused by how the retelling of their deeds has blurred fact and fiction, and some of them desperately wanting to embellish what they did in the belief that immortality may need a helpful shove now and then.

The roster is glittering—54 athletes in all, from A (Adderley, Herb and Alworth, Lance) to W (Ward, Rodger and Weaver, Earl).

There are ones we remember for their speed—Bullet Bob Hayes, maybe the greatest of all "world's fastest humans," and Bullet Bob Feller, whose fastball must have been at least Mach 3.

There are ones we remember for their grace—Willie Mays and Joe DiMaggio, tracking down line drives, Elgin Baylor and Oscar Robertson, who made basketball an art form.

There are ones we remember as quaint curiosities—Bruno Sammartino, who combined wrestling skills with thespian flair and packed arenas, and Bobby Riggs, who was con and hustle and guile and also just good enough to pluck a lot of pigeons clean.

They are all here, they and Rick Barry and Lou Brock, Don Budge and Roy Campanella, Leo Durocher and Walt Frazier, Gordie Howe and Bobby Hull, Jim Ryun and Warren Spahn—and the widows, too: Rachel Robinson and Ruth Owens, Vera Clemente and Martha Louis.

It is modestly billed as the largest assemblage of all-time great athletes in one place at one time. For once, that is as much truth as it is hyperbole.

What they all have in common is that they have been profiled on *Greatest Sports Legends*, the nationally syndicated TV program that will begin its 10th year with a special program that will be filmed tonight at a banquet at Bally's Park Place Casino Hotel.

The whole idea came to Berl Rotfeld, he says, when he was sitting in a Philadelphia bar, listening to other sports junkies involved in another of those insanely opinionated, passionately argued, hopelessly subjective debates about who was the best hitter of a baseball, the best shooter of a basketball, the fastest runner with a football.

Rotfeld had been a songwriter and knew the basics of production. The format was simple enough: a half-hour show, packed with lots of action footage and the athlete himself talking about what he did, how he did it, how it felt.

If Berl Rotfeld did that first program—on Hugh McElhenny, a marvelously elusive broken-field runner—on a shoestring, that shoestring has since become pure Gucci. Sports Legends Inc., of which Berl Rotfeld is president, is the stuff of conglomerates.

After seven hosts, nine seasons on the air and 99 shows, *Greatest Sports Legends* is an envied commodity, a hot property that has been remarkably durable in an industry in which lifespans are notoriously short. It is the longest-running sports show in TV syndication history.

And the onetime songwriter now presides over an empire—headquartered on City Avenue in Bala Cynwyd—that includes 43 of the top 50 U.S. TV markets, TV in more than 40 foreign countries, home videocassettes and videodiscs, and all sorts of spinoffs, including quiz games and books.

Rotfeld has rounded up more than half his documentary-interview subjects for a big bash here, a sort of reunion of a very special fraternity. Call it a gathering of eagles. Some of them have had their wings clipped. But there was a time when they all soared and, in a vicarious way, took us with them.

Letting Go:
The Struggle to Leave

JULY 2, 1989

Unlike the rest of us, who only have to deal with it once, athletes have to die twice. The second time is when they are hoisted up on six pairs of shoulders and carried away. The first time is when the skills that made them so exceptional begin to deteriorate and then finally desert them. When that happens, they die in public.

The first time is the toughest. We have that on good authority.

Muhammad Ali hunches over the bowl, almost in it, and spoons soup toward his mouth with trembling hands. It dribbles down his chin. Once, he had been so lithe and sleek, the ultimate matador, moving with such grace. Now, he can't feed himself soup.

When you have been king of the world, what do you remember most?

"I always wondered," he said in that whisper that makes you lean in close, "if I had kept on fighting, that maybe I wouldn't have gotten this sickness."

Even now, even with the extra weight, even with the uncontrollable tremors, he yearns for the competition. He was most alive when he could fight. Now that he isn't allowed to anymore, his eyes dull, his head settles on his chest in sad, desperate resignation.

He is left only with his dreams.

We have followed her from Ice Maiden to sedate matron, through marriage and divorce and remarriage, from teen icon to thirty-something wind-down.

Chris Evert, at 34: "Really, my only purpose since I was six years old was tennis."

That purpose is now gone.

In January, she announced that this would be her final year, capped by a farewell tour of Europe and the United States. Less than a month later, she had second thoughts. Then, at the French Open last month, she withdrew from an event she had won seven times.

She left the court and was heard to say to her husband, Andy Mill, tearfully: "I can't play anymore. My heart isn't in the game."

Now, she is back playing, at Wimbledon. Clearly, this leave-taking is one traumatic thing.

"I played so well early this year," she explained. "I thought, 'Well, it's still there.' An athlete has 10 or 15 quality years, and you feel you might as well milk it for as long as you can. When you've been on a pedestal, there is no way to go but down. People don't like to see you fall. But very few athletes retire on top, and if you've been a champion, you'd like to play a little past your prime."

A month ago, the best third baseman in history, tortured into sleepless agony at watching balls that he used to gobble up without thought or effort skip tauntingly past his frantic lunges, abruptly announced his retirement.

Mike Schmidt's immediate reaction was immense relief.

"I can't tell you how relieved I am," he said. "It's hard to put into words, but when you're used to doing something and being one of the best, then you see somebody replacing you at the top, you fight like hell against it. So I gave it six games. Seven. Eight. Nine. Ten. And it just wasn't there.

"When you get a disease, you can't tell the disease to just go away."

As with Chris Evert, the prospect of playing at a level, however slight, below the best in the world, was unimaginable for Mike Schmidt. Unbearable. Unacceptable.

He made his decision and says he is at peace with it. Evert wrestles still with hers, tangled in ambivalence. One day she wants to get out, the next she hits a forehand from memory and thinks maybe she should stay on.

And Muhammad Ali, once the best there was, spoons soup and fights the shakes and wonders whether, if he had kept on boxing, he might not have gotten this insidious disease that is killing him by inches.

At almost the exact moment that Mike Schmidt was walking out on his own accord, on his own terms, the oldest of the old pros was given his release.

"What's released mean? " Taylor John, age seven, asked his mother.

"It means Dad won't be pitching anymore," said Sally John of her husband, Tommy. "At least not for the Yankees."

He is 46. In his mind, he can pitch until he is 60.

"He probably will be able to pitch until he's 60," agreed Dallas Green, the Yankees' manager. "Whether he'll be able to get people out is something else."

John has 288 major-league victories. This was his 26th season in the bigs, making him the first player in baseball's modern history to last that long. Most athletes are thankful for a short career. But the longer they last, the longer they think they can last.

Is it any wonder that, in some secret corner of their minds, they begin to wonder if they can play forever?

A few days after Mike Schmidt walked out the door and Tommy John was shown the door, Kareem Abdul-Jabbar found himself on the doorstep. But he hasn't exactly taken that last stride over the threshold. He is spending this summer on tour, barnstorming abroad. And already there are stories about offers to him to play in Europe.

A million for another season. One more chance. One more season.

"It's what you're always looking for," said Tommy John, who understands better than any of us. "Just one more chance."

Just one more season.

One more, please. One more, and that will be it. For sure. Honest. Promise.

4

Football . . . Mass Times Speed Equals Ka-Boom!

Paterno: Old Fart

NOVEMBER 21, 2006

Penn State is playing football at Wisconsin and Joe Paterno is barking at the officials, railing against an injustice that he insists any fool can plainly see, and the cameras close in on his face of rage, and at one point, Craig James, an analyst for ABC-TV, refers to the icon of Happy Valley as an "old fart."

Excuse me. Old fart?

On behalf of O-Fs everywhere, permit me this succinct and most heartfelt rebuttal: "Up yours, Sonny."

Some of us have socks older than you.

Joe Paterno's odometer will click on 80 next month. In the O-F game, he was bowled over like 10 pins by two players the size of small continents in a sideline collision that broke one leg and ripped ligaments in the other. His response was to lurch back to his feet, try to limp it off and, cantankerous and grumpy to the end, impatiently wave away offers of assistance.

It took 20 minutes of coaxing and cajoling to get him to agree to leave the field, and then, hauled off in the meat wagon, his face was contorted in disgust, rather like Patton being forced to leave the field of battle.

He was hospitalized. A more impatient patient, we were told, you could not imagine. It was learned that a month earlier he had been run over by his own players, large and at full velocity, during practice. Three ribs were broken. He didn't miss a beat.

O-F, indeed.

One broken leg, one shredded knee and three broken ribs, and he continued to resist and persist.

One of his players, safety Anthony Scirrotto, who is roughly 60 years younger, said of his coach: "Even when he gets knocked down, he doesn't want to be helped up. He's got some bounce in his step."

Tight end Andrew Quarless, who was mortified to have been involved in both collisions, said Paterno lectured him even as he was scrambling to his feet after the Wisconsin hit: "We've got a game to win. Stay focused."

O-F, indeed.

He agreed, reluctantly but wanting to avoid the distraction his presence would cause, to miss the next game. The Nittany Lions trampled Temple, 47-0.

Speedball Derrick Williams said afterward: "He took a hit and he could still get up. That's the kind of determination Joe has. He fights. How could we do anything else?"

O-F? Ha!

Wayne Sebastianelli, Penn State's director of athletic medicine, who operated on Paterno, said: "To give you a sense of the physical and mental toughness of this guy, he had three fractured ribs and he never missed 10 seconds of practice. Not 10 seconds. He got knocked down, knocked the dust off his pants, and kept coaching."

Words to live by . . . especially if you're an O-F.

In the interest of at least a modicum of objectivity, it must be noted that in recent years, Paterno has done some things that made you cringe, said some things that made you wince, much of it chalked up to, uh, well, age.

Paterno himself, who has always been self-deprecating, might agree with this bit of T-shirt philosophy: "With age comes wisdom . . . but sometimes age comes alone."

Or another T-shirt offering: "Old age is not for sissies."

This is of particular interest in this particular moment in time because the O-F population in this country is about to mushroom. The baby boomers are closing in on that station in life when you can play connect-the-dots with your liver spots, when each morning you are greeted with a new twinge—"Hmmmm, haven't felt that one before"—when the trip from bed to bathroom is done in fits and starts, stop 'n' go, and when how long a minute lasts depends on which side of the bathroom door you're standing.

Old fartism can be surrendered to . . . or, you can rise up on your hind legs and defy, defy, defy.

It need not be feared.

I read somewhere that one advantage of reaching old fartism is that if you're ever involved in a hostage situation, at least you'll be among the first released.

The sustaining, affirming part of O-F-ism is that you have learned how, when and where to spend your energy. You hoard your passion for the really important moments.

Or, in another bit of T-shirt philosophy: "You can't help growing older, but you can help growing old."

Or, in this tale-with-a-moral:

One day an old bull and a young bull are out walking and they come to the crest of a hill, and there, spread out before them in the valley below, is a herd of female cows of all ages and sizes.

"Oh, wow!" says the eager young bull. "Let's run down there and get us one."

And the older, wiser bull says: "Let's walk down and get 'em all."

Now that's an old fart after my own heart.

Paterno:
A Championship at Last

JANUARY 2, 1983

New Orleans—Deliverance.

On a fog-shrouded evening of foreboding, Penn State seized at last what it had been denied for so long:

Deliverance.

Number one, the Holy Grail of collegiate football, will reside in 1983 in Happy Valley, that rural hamlet that has been home for a school and a coach who had become, perversely, as well-known for what they had not won as for what they had.

Afterward, after Penn State had outlasted gallant Georgia, 27-23, in a throbber last night, Joe Paterno accepted the victory ride atop his players' shoulders, the ride which many have imagined he has dreamed of, become obsessed over, for 17 years.

But it was not a cloud-hopping kind of ride. He seemed restrained. He has insisted that vindication, atonement, was not one of his needs.

A national championship, he said, would mean more to Penn State followers than to himself. Perhaps. But the blue-and-white bedecked zealots stopped their whooping and their celebration long enough to put out a raucous, crooning chant: "We want Joe. . . We want Joe."

They didn't get him. He remained inside to talk with the team that had given itself and the school:

Deliverance.

So now, alongside all those Lambert Trophies, alongside the mementos of 44 consecutive nonlosing teams, goes the national championship.

Number one is not official, of course. Not yet. The ballots of those who vote in the wire-service polls are due today. Southern Methodist, with only a tie marring its otherwise perfect record, would like to debate the matter. But when number two beats number one, head-to-head, the voting should be a formality.

Indeed, there was no doubt in the Sugar Bowl's mind.

While a sullen, persistent rain continued to splatter outside, inside the Superdome the scoreboard flashed its electronic coronation: "Penn State . . . National Champions.

Underneath the scoreboard, Penn State players ran through gauntlets of high-fives, their bodies in spasmodic, impromptu victory dances, disco steps of ecstasy, and of:

Deliverance.

In this current sports calendar, we seem to be making a habit of shedding monkeys. Last March, in this same building, Dean Smith, the basketball coach at North Carolina, had won his first national title, the only meaningful bauble that had ever eluded him.

And now comes Joe Paterno, like Smith, esteemed, lionized, but minus a number one. Perhaps this was not so much a slur as it was a wishing by the fans that both Smith and Paterno somehow deserved national championships. Smith got his and now Paterno has his.

Still, Paterno brushed aside the notion that he should lead a chorus of "Free at last, free at last."

"I don't think there is anything to be relieved of," Paterno said. "I felt satisfied all those years when we won them all. It wasn't my fault in those years that the votes weren't there."

And he would admit, under questioning, that he had a premonition that this would be the year of:

Deliverance.

"I just kind of felt it would happen this time," he said. "There has been a kind of chemistry on this team all year long. They're the kind of players who, when they lose their poise, have a way of getting it back."

They lost that poise a couple of times last night, and they did recover it. Twice they had left Georgia choking on their exhaust; and twice they checked the rear-view mirror, and there were the Bulldogs gaining. Each time, Penn State pulled away again. That is the mark of championship teams.

Number one was achieved, fittingly, in the same arena where it had been denied to the Nittany Lions four years ago. They had been atop the polls for the first time in history then, and had gone down to bitter defeat against Alabama.

The Sugar Bowl had held only sour memories for Penn State. It had sent three teams here previously, and all three had limped home, losers, and unable to score more than seven points in a game.

They scored that many in the first $2^1/_2$ minutes last night. They got another touchdown and two field goals in the second quarter, and with less than a minute left in the first half, they had bolted to a 20-3 lead.

That seemed commanding, secure, enough to exorcise the ghosts of Sugar Bowls past, enough to guarantee:

Deliverance.

And then again, maybe not. For Georgia, which ranked 96th among the 97 Division I-A teams in passing this year, went 66 yards in 39 seconds, on five plays, all through the air, to cut that Penn State lead in half.

A TD just before intermission, when you are behind, is the biggest emotional supercharger in football. Sure enough, Georgia, revived now, came out and took the second-half kickoff and scored again, and it was 20-17.

A Sugar Bowl record crowd of 78,124 was in a foaming frenzy, Georgia backers raging and generating more momentum, Penn State backers pleading for the dam to hold.

Amid all that din, you could almost hear the clanking chains of the ghosts of Sugar Bowls past, haunting Penn State. Was there to be another memorable collapse?

But the ghosts were quieted when Gregg Garrity, a wide receiver running a sideline streak, launched himself in a spectacular swan dive and gathered in a 48-yard TD pass from Todd Blackledge as he made a belly landing in the end zone.

It was 27-17, Penn State, but even that was not safe.

Georgia would rumble back and score another TD and then would go for two points on the conversion. If successful, it would be 27-25, Penn State, and Georgia would then be able to preserve its perfect season with a field goal.

The only surprise would have been if someone other than Herschel Walker had been given the ball.

There were no surprises.

Neither were there any points.

Walker took a pitch and tried to sweep around the right side. Penn State's defense had strung it out. Walker tried to cut back. He was stuffed, smothered by four defenders.

It was 27-23, and Georgia would need a touchdown. It would not get it. It would not even get a chance.

Penn State wrung the clock dry, all but six seconds' worth, and those evaporated as Ralph Giacomarro's punt, safely launched over an all-out, 11-man Georgia rush, bounded toward the end zone.

The clock had reached zeros before the ball stopped spinning.

Deliverance.

"Certainly, it feels good," Paterno said, "but it will probably feel better when it sets in, when we have time to stop and think about it "

And to savor it.

"I think we beat three or four of the top teams in the country during this season, and certainly we should be number one. When the number one and number two teams play, and the number two team wins, I certainly think they should move up."

They did the last time there was a number one vs. number two shootout. That was right here, the 1979 Sugar Bowl. It was the fifth time number one had played number two since the polls began, and it became the only time number one had lost.

The only time, that is, until last night. And until:

Deliverance.

Paterno: Chilling Autumn . . . Happily-Ever-Aftering

NOVEMBER 4, 2004

This has come to be excruciating to watch.

A prideful man, a stalwart man of dignity and moral worth, an obstinate man, a fiercely competitive man, a man who has spent more than half a century sparring with windmills, a man who has given his life to a university, a man who is truly a man for all seasons . . . this man now struggles with the autumn of his life.

Joseph Vincent Paterno and Pennsylvania State University have been yoked for 55 years. Hard to tell which one loves the other more.

But at the place to which Paterno has devoted his passion and his imagination, his crusader's zeal and his philanthropist's great heart, he now does harm. He may not realize it; indeed, he must not realize it because the last thing he would want to do is inflict pain on the place that has been, with his considerable help, his Camelot.

But, in Camelot, there is always happily-ever-aftering.

And these days, the rain falls cold and hard on Happy Valley. Another winter of discontent is descending like a shroud over Mount Nittany.

It shouldn't be this way.

But you get the uneasy and queasy feeling that it has crossed the line now, and that it can only end badly, and it is a terrible, horrible feeling, as if you have been gut-shot. And you hope you are wrong.

Here is the conundrum: The chorus clamoring for him to be led away grows weekly, in volume and in voices. They all send up variations on the same theme. But he wants things to end gloriously, because he feels such an obligation to the place, and he wants this so badly that he has convinced himself that he can still effect the grand turnaround, and that it is his solemn duty not to leave until he has.

And you hope, mightily, that he can.

But there is precious little supportive evidence.

He keeps saying the Nittany Lions are close. Close to being good. Which is still a long, long way from where they once were.

All the numbers are grim, and combined form a definite, distressing trend: 32 losses in 56 games since 2000. The fourth season in the last five with more losses than wins. Only one Big Ten Conference win in the last

13 starts. Only five wins in the last 21 games. More unsettling and more telling is that those wins came against opponents like Kent State, Akron and Temple.

Against opponents of even modest stature, the Nittany Lions are man-handled at the line of scrimmage and treated with such a lack of respect that, two weeks ago, Iowa deliberately took a safety, even knowing that all Penn State would need to beat the Hawkeyes was a field goal. In effect, Iowa was saying: We know you can't score on us.

Gallingly, the Nittany Lions couldn't, and lost by the unlikely and embarrassing score of 6-4.

Once a man of unshakable and implacable resoluteness, Paterno strikes you as floundering and unsure at times, particularly when he says he wishes he knew what was wrong, and, even more, how to fix it.

"I have no magic bullet," he said the other day.

This senior class will have gone to one bowl game. In the sweet used-to-be, the Lions went every year.

A bunch of us would meet with him on Friday nights and, teasingly, we'd ask: Which bowl this time, Joe? And he would rebut: The holidays are nice up here; you ought to come up.

The joke has become reality.

Inevitably, any discussion about the man includes the matter of age. He will be 78 next month. The school extended his contract for four years last year.

At times, when he is flailing his arms and railing against the officials or offering sour wine at a media conference, he seems a crotchety old man. And then at a pep rally, he can transform into a tent-meeting-revival evangelist and have the crowd howling in his hand, and at such moments you marvel at his energy and think: Please let me have that much juice when I'm 77.

The other day, he was asked if he thought he deserved to return next season. He replied tartly: "I don't appreciate that question, to be honest, after 55 years here."

But it was a question that needed both asking and answering.

Of course he feels a sense of entitlement. He should, for all he has done.

He doesn't need me to defend him, Lord knows.

But I wish I had an answer. Because in 48 years in this business, having hung around mountebanks and charlatans, preeners and peacocks, unassuming winners, gracious losers, and doers of deeds both great and small, with those who made it and those who fell agonizingly short, he is still first in my roll call of respect.

For that, I hope happily-ever-aftering is still possible.

Cappy: Something for Joey

N ew York—It was one of those nights when a guy who rents tuxedos for
a living does six months worth of business in a couple of hours.

There was a lot of crushed velvet and satin and diamonds, and you
knew a few weeks worth of salary went into some of those gowns. This
was the Grand Ballroom of the New York Hilton and it was $50 a head, a
very posh, very swank affair, not one of those things you could just wan-
der into off the street to get warm or just browse around till the rain
stopped.

There was a long, glittering dais up in front, and sitting around it were
maybe 100 Distinguished Guests. They capitalized the D and the G, see,
so us hamburger types would be impressed and know this was real filet
mignon stuff.

Well, there were all manner of great and near-great athletes, and a few
so-so's, too. And there were 21 former winners of the Heisman Trophy.
And the new Vice President of the United States was there, too, and of
course, there were all sorts of secret-agent types scurrying around.

Joe Paterno was there, and so was Bill Sullivan, the owner of the New
England Patriots, who offered the Penn State coach roughly one million
dollars to try the pro game prior to the 1973 season.

"There's a man on this dais," Paterno told the assembled crowd, "who
offered me an awful lot of money about a year ago, and I said no. Now, I'm
glad I turned him down, because no amount of money would have meant
as much to me as the last year and being part of John Cappelletti's life."

There were close to 4,000 people there in all, a lot of them trying to
impress one another, some of them trying to strut while they were sitting,
but when it was all over, the whole big evening belonged to a family from
Upper Darby, Mr. and Mrs. John Cappelletti and their daughter and their
four sons, who are what families are supposed to be all about.

Because after all the speeches and the introductions, the Cappelletti's
21-year-old son, John, got up to officially accept the Heisman Trophy as
the outstanding college football player in the country this year.

The award is very big in a lot of ways. When John Cappelletti got done
talking, that award had gotten much, much bigger.

For the last two years, John Cappelletti had done a lot of heroic things
on a football field for Penn State. He has carried the ball as many as 41

times in a single afternoon, and gotten stomped and butted and clawed and punched and generally very roughed up.

Thursday night he stood up and swallowed very hard and made about a 10-minute speech that nobody can write because a typewriter, no matter how magic it may be, doesn't have a heart.

At the end, John Cappelletti had thanked a lot of people. And then he dedicated the most coveted award in sports to his 11-year-old brother.

His name is Joey Cappelletti and he has leukemia.

It was discovered six years ago. They started taking Joey to Children's Hospital in Philadelphia and there were 46 other kids in his group. Joey is the only one still alive.

At times he has been in a coma for weeks. He has to take shots every other day. And very painful bone–marrow tests, too. And doctors keep reminding the Cappelletti's—gently—that any new drug they try will only prolong; it will not cure.

There was no easy way for John Cappelletti to tell the people in the Grand Ballroom about Joey. It was tougher than any power sweep he ever ran.

But on this, his night, John Cappelletti explained he wanted to do something to let Joey know how he felt.

"He never complains, he never asks why; he accepts it but he refuses to give up," John Cappelletti said.

"He's been through so much that it makes me feel what I go through—and then the rewards I get in return—well, it's all so small compared to him, and…"

It was tough to continue. It tough to put into words what he meant.

And John Cappelletti cried. He broke down and wept unashamedly, and grown men and women in the audience wept with him.

"Joey has been an inspiration for me," he said.

But out there in the audience, surrounded by all those dressed-up grown-ups, Joey Cappelletti smiled to let his brother know he understood. Joey Cappelletti is far, far wiser than his 11 years.

John Cappelletti told everyone he had tried to look back to see if there was an ingredient, a formula, a common thread that had run through his life that had made him a Heisman Trophy winner.

He said he owed a lot to a lot of people. He mentioned his teammates. And his coaches, like Joe Paterno ("he is as interested in me as a person as he is as a football player"). And his high school coach, Jack Gottschalk, who died last summer ("when the season was over, he didn't just disappear, he tried to get guys into college and it didn't matter if they had been All-Staters or fourth-stringers; in 43 years he accomplished more than a lot of people do in a lifetime").

And he mentioned his other brothers (Marty and Mike, and his sister Jeannie) "who were always there, who were behind me when things were rough, too, not just in the good times."

And then he looked at his parents.

"They have five kids but they always have treated us as equals. They never pushed you into anything, but whatever you did, they were always there.

"They are strong people."

He smiled. "And they are very, very tough."

You know that just by listening to John Cappelletti, or looking at Joey Cappelletti.

When John Cappelletti sat down, there were a lot of wet eyes and the applause lasted a long time. The people realized they had seen something very special. Something bigger than any trophy ever made. It's called love.

Without a Victory,
But Winners Anyway

DECEMBER 4, 2003

To play football for Army or for Navy is to be told this: All we want is all that you have.

On Saturday, near sundown, they will play each other for the 104th time. There is no other rivalry quite like it.

From the playing field, they will go to a higher calling.

They know the drill, understand the inevitability of the oath they have taken: All will give some, some will give all.

No Division I team has ever lost 13 times in one season. Army goes into this game 0-12. You might think by now that they would be numb, and couldn't feel the losing. You would be wrong.

You might think that all that losing makes them losers. You would be grievously wrong.

Ohhhhhhhhhhhh-and-12.

How must that feel?

"I cry after every game," he admits. "I don't wish that feeling on anyone."

But you keep on, don't you? You go to practice every day anyway, don't you? You pour yourself into it. Because you are certain that this is the week when the losing will stop. This will be the game when it all turns around.

"Yes, sir. If you don't feel that way," he says, "then you have no chance."

Name: Kent, Ryan Evan. Senior, West Point. Hometown: Woodbury, New Jersey. Co–captain, Brave Old Army Team. Outside linebacker now, field artillery soon. He sits before you straight as a bayonet.

In high school, he was an option quarterback and won two state championships. At the Point, they asked him to move to defense. He did and became a tackling machine.

In the last two seasons, he and his teammates have played 24 games, and they have lost 23 of them. They soldier on anyway, not an ounce of give-up in them. The losing, they find, bonds them rather than dividing them.

"We're a very tight group," he says; "0-and-12 is no fun. But we have each other. We're members of a very special brotherhood."

Ohhhhhhhhhhhh-and-12.

How must that feel?

"It hurts. We know how much it hurts," he says. "We've been in that situation ourselves. Empathy? Sure. You can't be human and not feel that. I'm sure they don't want any sympathy. I'm sure they're out there practicing as hard as anyone."

Name: Candeto, Craig Louis. Senior, United States Naval Academy. Hometown: Orange City, Florida. Co–captain, Navy. Quarterback now, jet jockey soon. He sits before you, blond and toothsome, with just the right amount of cocky-cool.

He looks like he could land a jet on the deck of an aircraft carrier, which is what he wants to do. Or run through Army, which he did last year, scoring six touchdowns in a 58-12 rout.

"I guarantee I'll be a marked man this year," he says, smiling.

Candeto has led Navy to a 7-4 record this season and a bowl game. But in his first three seasons at Annapolis, Navy was 1-10, 0-10, 2-10.

"We know what Army's going through," he says. "Inside, you can't help but bleed a little for them. After all, when this game is over, we'll all become the same band of brothers."

Ohhhhhhhhhhhh-and-12.

How must that feel?

"You can't feel sorry for yourself," he says. "What's kept us together is each other. We play for the coaches. We play for the Corps. But mostly we play for each other. No one wants to let down the guy next to him."

Name: Woody, Clinton Ray. Senior, West Point. Hometown: Hayesville, North Carolina. Co–captain, Army. Wide receiver now, helicopter pilot soon. He will have to scrunch up and fold himself into the chopper, for he is six-foot-six. It makes him easy to find, though. He has caught two dozen passes this season.

In his four seasons, Army has won five games. And lost 41. The losing sets in like a dull toothache after a time. But you never learn to accept it.

"Would I do the last four years all over again?" he repeats the question. "Absolutely. You're not in this by yourself. You're a part of something so much bigger than yourself. And football is just that, football. We know what's ahead. It's why we came here."

In four years, he never missed a practice. Not one.

Ohhhhhhhhhhhh-and-12.

How must that feel?

"Like you're all hollow inside," he says. "Like something just got sucked out of you. But you never think about quitting. No, all you think is to-morrow. We'll go out there, and we'll get 'em tomorrow."

Name: Carthan, Eddie Charles Jr. Senior, United States Naval Academy. Hometown: Donalsonville, Georgia. Co–captain, Navy. Linebacker now, sailor soon. He sits before you with the puffed chest and ax-handle shoulders that are forged in the weight room. But there is no armor against the hurt of losing.

"Two years ago, we were where Army is now," he says. "Wondering if you'd ever win again. You feel like you let so many people down. But you go on, because you love the game and because you develop a love for the guy next to you.

"And then, this week, the week of Army–Navy, you get e-mails from all over the world, from Japan and Iraq, all over, because they keep track of you no matter where they're stationed . . . and that, that brings you back to the real world."

At the Point, you are given the chance to bail out. Before you begin your junior year, you can drop out, walk away, no questions asked.

On this team that is Ohhhhhhhhhhhh-and-12, there are 44 cadets who, when presented with that opportunity to quit, declined the offer. Respectfully but emphatically.

You would bet everything that not one of them regrets his choice.

The Real Drama Came
After the Game

DECEMBER 7, 2003

And so once again the cannons had fallen silent, the drums were a disappearing echo, the moon was fat and full, and the two teams whose rivalry commands history were coming together in the dank December chill, the winners weeping, the losers weeping, fierce football foes but now fast friends, tethered to each other forever by a common cause.

Army went first, as protocol and tradition insists the losers must, the players dutifully lining up to face the Corps of Cadets, there to sing the alma mater of West Point. And directly behind them, at respectful attention, stood the victorious Navy team.

And then Navy was spinning around and whooping across the wind-lashed field to celebrate before the howling Brigade of Midshipmen, and Army was right behind, making what surely must be the longest walk there is to be made in sports, there to return the favor, to stand while the Naval Academy alma mater was sung.

Of all the rituals and rites in our sports, this moment remains the one that continues to touch you in the deepest part.

In a cynical, jaded age, when taunting and trashing and self-celebration threaten to suck the joy from sport, here is always a reminder of that quaint concept known as sportsmanship, thought by some to have gone irretrievably out of style.

Army and Navy. Oh, not the game itself, even though it sometimes makes magic. But the ending, when the two accord each other a full measure of respect, that is when something begins to leak from your eyes.

How fitting, and how ironic, that this salute to your opponent is brought to us courtesy of the two most bitter of rivals, by warrior patriots, by our best and brightest.

Army and Navy played for the 104th time yesterday. Played in the Linc for the first time. Played in brutal cold and goalpost-swaying wind. Played the game that each one of them would give everything to play, even to the point of . . . well, Josh Smith, the starting free safety for Navy, woke up doubled over in agony Wednesday.

Acute appendicitis.

There would be no Army–Navy game for him.

His response was to ask for a second opinion. And that opinion was: "Oh yeah, that baby's got come out, and now!"

And Josh Smith's response to that was: "I want a third opinion."

Which he got and which turned out to be exactly the same as the second and the first, and Josh Smith said . . . well, this time he didn't get a chance to say anything because they said to him, sternly this time: "No more opinions, Josh."

Given the chance, you suspect that Josh Smith would have removed his own appendix, with a rusty razor blade yet, for the chance to play, for the chance to stand before the Brigade and sing the alma mater in victory, and to stand at respectful attention before the Army Corps of Cadets.

His team won. Army played its guts out, kept it close, but Navy pulled methodically away, its triple–option offense piling up 359 yards rushing on the way to a 34-6 victory. Army could not stop the Navy fullback Kyle Eckel, who grew up in South Philly, and who kept butting his gold helmet that is pitted with gouges and dents through the Army defense.

And thus ended a season of ignominy for Army.

It is now the first Division I football team to lose 13 games in one season.

Thirteen losses, no wins.

Think that demoralized them?

"I'd rather play for this team than any team in the country," said the outside linebacker, Ryan Kent, a co–captain. The tears were fresh on his face.

With only three minutes and 36 seconds left in the game, and down by 28 points, with all hope of victory gone, Army rushed to call a timeout just before Navy was to punt. Rather than permit the clock to hurry along and mercifully get a foregone conclusion over with, Army chose to prolong its misery.

Why?

Because to surrender, no matter what the score, no matter what the circumstances, is unthinkable.

Unthinkable on a football field, and even more unthinkable on a battlefield.

Remember the Point's admonition to all cadets, that there are only three acceptable answers no matter what the question is: Yes, sir. No, sir. And no excuse, sir.

By 11 yesterday morning, more than five hours before kickoff, a small army of parka-bundled civilian workers was determinedly hacking away at the ice-encrusted Linc, scraping and shoveling, chopping and salting, all the while knowing they were fighting a losing battle, for the wind was blowing the still-falling snow sideways.

Machines bigger than tanks cleared the parking lots, and did so with a relentless efficiency. But inside the new stadium, the aisle steps remained stubborn and unyielding, and by night they were glazed over, the footing so treacherous you thought they ought to be named Litigation Alleys. For here, in ambush, were lawsuits waiting to happen.

By eight last night, the workers were manicuring the playing field, seeding and rolling, and its scars seemed to be minuscule. Today will be the first litmus test for the Linc, its first turn as foul–weather host, and, as luck would have it, this is also the first high-stakes game there, the Eagles and the Dallas Cowboys about to decide the NFC East.

They have a tough act to follow.

On-Field Enemies,
Off-Field Brothers

DECEMBER 5, 2004

After the rolling thunder of the jet fighters and their shattering flyover, after the ceiling-fan whump-whump-whump of the choppers, after the sky-skiing parachutists had stuck their landings on the playing field, after the President had presided over the coin toss, after they had, for $3^1/_2$ hours, hammered away at each other, and after the cannons' last smoke rings had evaporated in the crisp December gloaming, they took off their golden helmets and they saluted each other, warrior patriots honoring their foes.

There were tears. There always are.

There is ritual in war and there is ritual in football, and almost always the best part of Army-Navy is after the game has ended and the bitterest of enemies exchange alma maters and everlasting respect.

And so, as is custom and tradition, both teams, golden helmets under their arms, stood at attention before the Corps of Cadets from West Point yesterday, for in this ritual it is the losers who go first. And then they crossed the field at Lincoln Financial Field, both squads, to stand before the midshipmen from Annapolis, victors valiant yet again, 42-13.

They have played each other in parts of three centuries now, played in the comfort and ease and prosperous flush of peace, when we have dozed on the front porch, Sunday-dinner-sated and rocking-chair complacent.

And they have played when the bombs have dropped and the folded flags have been given to sobbing widows, presented at graveside with a solemn, inadequate condolence: "On behalf of a grateful nation . . . ."

They have played each other 105 times now and the ledger is perfectly balanced, as square as such a glorious rivalry should be: Army 49 wins, Navy 49 wins, seven ties.

But it is Navy dominating now, Navy winning another easy one yesterday, winning by 29 and pulling away; Navy winning five of the last six, Navy winning the last three, and by the horribly lopsided margin of 134-31.

And Army, what of Army? Army needs to regroup. Army needs, to paraphrase the anonymous poet, to resolve to do this: I think I shall lay me down here and bleed for a little while, and then arise and fight some more.

And Navy, what of Navy? Navy is on quite a nice little run now, having effected an admirable turnaround. There was a time when this senior class was 2-20 as freshmen and sophomores. As juniors and seniors, they are 17-7 and will be playing in a second straight bowl game. An example to inspire Army.

The middies are led by a punishing fullback and an adventurous safety.

Kyle Eckel is the fullback. He runs as if he ought to be hitched to a Budweiser wagon. He trampled Army for 179 rushing yards and his 25th career touchdown. He also made news by actually losing yards on a run. He has done that four times—in well over 400 carries.

Navy runs a triple-option offense and it all begins with the 240-pound Eckel. They send him barreling into the middle again and again and again: Eck-Eck-Eck . . . three-four-five times in a row, and when the defense has been drawn in and massed for his next assault, quarterback Aaron Polanco slips the ball back out of Eckel's belly and decides which of the options to take—run it himself, pitch to a trailer, or pass.

It becomes such a simple game when you have a player the opponent must stop and cannot.

Josh Smith is the safety. He led the middies in tackles the last three seasons. He roams the range like a lobo. He swallowed up an Army pass yesterday and ran it back 67 yards for a touchdown, and this was especially sweet because he had not been able to play in last year's game. He had an emergency appendectomy. He had it three days before the game.

And he asked to play anyway. The doctor said no. He asked for a second opinion, and got it: No. He asked for a third and got it: No. It was suggested that, given the chance, he would have performed the surgery himself. He did not disagree.

Josh Smith is going to be in the Marines, and that isn't much of a surprise. He plans to become a jet jockey, and that's even less of a surprise.

The headlines over the last week have spoken ominously of further buildup of American troops in Iraq and Afghanistan. Some who played in this game could be asked to give the last full measure. Once they graduate, they know the pact that awaits: All will give some, some will give all.

"You know the drill, you know the deal," Polanco said. "We're blessed to play football now. But you know what you signed up for."

With 35 seconds left yesterday, behind by 29, down to fourth and 14 at its own 20, as hopeless as hopeless gets, Army spent its final timeout. There are a lot of things possible in football, but a 30-point play isn't among them. No matter. What mattered was Army's refusal to give up, no matter how hopeless the circumstances.

"They'll get better," Polanco said. "They'll get it turned around."

Respect for an opponent. Such a quaint concept.

"We'll be enemies on the field," Polanco had said before the game, "but when all is said and done, we're one. We are a brotherhood."

This was the 78th time that Army and Navy have played each other in our city. Some of those venues now are, like autumn fields of poppies, no more than wilted memories: the cavernous Municipal Stadium, later re-named JFK; Franklin Field, a grand old dinosaur where, once upon a time, Army-Navy held the whole country enthralled; and Veterans Stadium, now reduced to sand dunes of rubble and reminiscence.

The Army-Navy game will remain in Philadelphia five of the next six years.

The privilege is all ours.

Favre: A Man Possessed

There is no manual for this, no textbook to study, no playbook to memorize.

There is no right way to grieve, no wrong way to mourn.

There is only what works for you.

So when we lose a loved one, we stumble about until we find what seems to fit, what seems to feel right for us, what we can draw around ourselves for warmth and comfort.

For Brett Favre, playing a football game the night after his father died is what felt right.

He ended up playing the game of his life.

And as you watched it, and him, every moment you have ever spent with your children, and your grandchildren, came flooding back. Every game of catch. Every bedtime story read. Every soccer game driven to. Every bit of homework agonized over. All of it, all of it that binds us and bonds us forever . . . mothers and sons, fathers and daughters, all the things we fumble to find the words for, all the things that, in the end, make everything else matter less than one minuscule grain of sand on a very large beach.

This all came in the midst of what is always such an emotional holiday anyway, when the ache of loss feels especially sharp and keen, when those who are no longer with us seem close by somehow, and here was this quarterback honoring the memory of the man who had been both his father and his coach by doing what he was sure the old man wanted.

Indeed, at one point in the game, one of Brett Favre's receivers, Javon Walker, said to him: "You know, your dad is having a hell of a time watching the way you're playing."

Against this, on *Monday Night Football*, the Oakland Raiders had no chance, no chance at all. Brett Favre was a man possessed. You swore you saw a bolt of blue flame arc from him to the rest of the Green Bay Packers, and they, too, played with an inspired, unstoppable fury. By intermission, Favre had played a statistically perfect game. The NFL has no higher quarterback rating than what he compiled in the first half as he passed for 311 yards and four touchdowns.

But even more electric was the way he played, with a sandlot joy, turned into a kid again, running free, laughing in the sun, rearing back and flinging the ball a country mile, certain that his receiver would outleap the defenders, sometimes as many as three of them, because this was a thing meant to be, a night on which he could do no wrong, in a game that would take on a life of its own and pass into lore and legend.

For one night, the field became Brett Favre's refuge.

And then, yesterday, in the lyrically named Mississippi town of Pass Christian, on Christmas Eve, Irvin Favre, who had died at the age of 58, was buried. The father of Brett Favre had suffered a heart attack while driving along the dusty Mississippi back roads, his pickup truck ending up in a ditch.

It fell to Deanna, Brett's wife, to take on the wrenching duty of making the phone call to her husband. She couldn't.

Instead, she called Doug Pederson, Favre's backup, on Pederson's cell phone. The same Doug Pederson so many of us roasted the first year of Andy Reid's coaching tenure with the Eagles. All you need to know about Doug Pederson is that he was the one Deanna Favre trusted and turned to in a terrible time, and it was Doug and Jeannie Pederson whom the Favres asked to fly home with them.

"Every game since the fifth grade," Favre said, referring to how often his father had seen him play.

And his father was his high school coach, too, and, yes, he was always harder on his own son than on the rest of them, which is almost always the way it is with fathers and sons, especially in such situations.

All that you need to know about Irvin Favre is that, even though he had a son who could throw a football through a car wash without it getting wet, he had other kids, too, other players' well-being and development to tend to, and some of them were very good at running the ball.

So, Irvin Favre installed the wishbone.

His son remembers telling him: "I'll never get to the pros this way, Dad."

But, of course, he did.

And when Brett Favre finally does retire, his next stop will be Canton, Ohio, and the Hall of Fame, and on that hot July day when he is inducted, he will feel, again, his father close by.

That game Monday night was number 205 in a row for Brett Favre, which is, by several city blocks, a record for a position fraught with peril. For 14 years, they have tried to hurt him enough so that he cannot play. No matter what they have broken, he has always played.

This time, what was broken cannot be splinted or casted.

He played not for the record, but for his team, which is all-out trying to reach the playoffs, and for the man who coached him and loved him and drove him and hugged him.

Wesley Walls, one of the Packers who catches Brett Favre's hissing spirals, said: "He played an amazing game for us, and we all felt we had to do the same for him."

The Packers' coach, Mike Sherman, said: "We were close as a team before, but now we're even closer. We can't change the events of the last 24 hours, but those events have changed us."

Some of our games are silly and many are irrelevant, and a lot of what we fret over is foolish. But every entrancing once in a while, one of them brings us a moment for reminding and for remembering.

Every once in a while, it's Christmas.

Riverfront: When Hell
Really Did Freeze Over

JANUARY 11, 1982

Cincinnati—And so we arrived at last at that apocalyptic day that we have been warned about for lo these many years. This was the day that hell finally did freeze over.

Outside the stadium, the Ohio River bubbled and frothed like some caldron deep in the bowels of Hades. Great white clouds of steam rose in surrealistic billows.

Those with a scientific bent tried to be reassuring. Vaporization, they said soothingly. Nothing more than the water being warmer than the air. Maybe, but they weren't fooling us. We knew. The river was on fire, that's what it was. A most foul and sinister omen. Repent, sinner. Doomsday is at hand.

At kickoff, the temperature was minus nine. The wind, a Siberian rage, was slashing in from the north at 35 m.p.h. The wind-chill factor was minus 59. It is a numbing number, incomprehensible really, because there is nothing in human experience to measure against it.

In the stands, the loonies trembled in paroxysms of uncontrollable shivering beneath their thermal layers, and they lit charcoal braziers and stuck their booted feet into the flaming coals in a vain effort to torch their circulation.

In the press box, a cup of coffee slipped from the deadened fingers of a writer. The scalding liquid splashed onto the cold concrete floor and, within minutes, congealed into a frozen puddle.

And down in the locker rooms, when it was over, the players peeled off their armor and padding and then began to strip away their makeshift insulation . . . arctic underwear, pantyhose, plastic trash bags and gooey gobs of Vaseline; it was like watching the exhumation of a platoon of mummies.

Against this backdrop, they played a football game here yesterday. For the AFC championship; that's AFC as in Absolutely Freezing Cold, or AFC as in Abominably Frigid Conditions, or AFC as in Astoundingly Frosted Cruelty.

There have been, down through the years of the NFL, some memorably frigid playoff games. Green Bay against the Giants in 1962, when it was so cold that today there is precious little footage for the archives, the

film having been destroyed by the weather even before it could be rushed
to the lab. Green Bay again, against Dallas in 1967, Bart Starr skating behind Jerry Kramer's block, treacherous inches over a frozen tundra. And
last year, Oakland at Cleveland, when sweat beaded players' faces one moment, crusted them in icicles the next.

But this was the worst. By acclamation and by consensus of those who
had survived those earlier polar expeditions, this was the worst.

"I can never remember having been so cold in my entire life," said Forrest Gregg, the coach of the winners. Gregg, remember, was a participant
in that Green Bay–Dallas glacier war.

It was so bad yesterday that the game almost wasn't played. Certainly,
San Diego wishes it never had been. Air Coryell never had a chance. The
Chargers could no more have won yesterday than a penguin could fly off
its iceberg and winter in Maui.

League officials awakened before dawn, scraped peepholes through the
frost on the inside of their hotel room windows, and wondered, fleetingly,
if the humane thing would be to call for a postponement. They lay back
down, however, and, sure enough, in a few moments that feeling passed.

There was a TV commitment, after all, and the Super Bowl was waiting out there, only two weeks away. Throw off all those schedules only to
save a few thousand people from becoming instant popsicles? Unthinkable. So, in a conscience-soothing gesture, the league announced that it
had consulted with a Dr. Ralph Goldman of the Army Research Institute
of Environmental Medicine.

It said that the good doctor had passed on some cold-weather survival
knowledge to the trainers for the Bengals and the Chargers. It may or may
not be significant that no one ever said whether the good doctor advised
against playing. The implication was that he said things would be just fine.
In fact, for all we know, he may have said something like: "Good grief, are
you guys nuts? Play football in this? Yeah, it's safe; about as safe as skinny-
dipping in the Bering Strait."

Whatever, they played. And the Bengals won in a crush, 27-7, and it
wasn't nearly that close.

The Chargers, who had given us that heroically memorable overtime
win against Miami eight days before, were down, 10-0, before their an-
tifreeze had a chance to kick in. Remember that they had played last in the
Orange Bowl, where the heat and humidity had combined for conditions
that felt like 84 degrees. Now they were lining up in minus 59. That is a
rather significant swing of 143 degrees.

And so they remain the classically flawed team, so utterly entertaining
to watch but so self-destructive, inevitably perishing by their own sword,
the forward pass.

Both teams, of course, took the obligatory approach, rightfully contending that weather was a trauma both had to endure. But despite all their protestations, it was obvious that the weather was a factor, and it was equally obvious that the Bengals were clearly more prepared, mentally and emotionally, to cope with it than were the Chargers.

"The strategy," said Bengals strong safety Bobby Kemp, "was to try to hit their receivers hard early, because cold weather affects hard hits even more."

Intimidated or not, San Diego's three 1,000-yard catchers—Kellen Winslow, Wes Chandler and Charlie Joiner—combined for only a dozen receptions for 167 yards and one score. Such stats are a routine day for any one of them, but hardly the smoldering ruins the three of them are accustomed to leaving.

But then the weather, especially the wind, may have disrupted the Chargers' quarterback, Dan Fouts, more than it did the receivers.

"I don't think they were affected any more than we were," said Bengals linebacker Reggie Williams, "except for Fouts. This wasn't the Fouts we had seen in game films. Forrest Gregg had told us beforehand that we weren't the first team to have to play in cold weather, and we wouldn't be the last."

"We tried to prepare them for the weather as best we could," Gregg said. "I think a real key was the way Blair Bush (the Bengals' center) and Kenny Anderson handled the ball. There were no fumbled snaps, and all those little things become more important in playoffs. You have to be careful with the ball."

The Bengals were; the Chargers weren't. The Chargers turned it over four times, the Bengals only once. Fouts threw two interceptions; Anderson threw none.

Make no mistake, however. The Bengals deserved this. They scored in every quarter. They scored with the wind and against the wind. They cashed in on turnovers and they generated long scoring drives.

And when they had built the commanding lead, they could work on the clock behind the pile-driving runs of fullback Pete Johnson, who is an earthquake on legs.

So, in the 14th year of their existence, the Bengals are bound for the Super Bowl. The team whose fans were once so disgruntled that they called the stadium "Neverfront" instead of Riverfront have seen Gregg whip a squad with tons of talent and a balky temperament into shape.

"We've always had the horses here," Pete Johnson said. "But it was always something holding us back, an injury here, a big mistake there. Now we've got it together, and I'd like to say it feels good, but I'm still so cold I can't feel anything."

Ah yes, back to the cold.

The AFC title game yesterday demonstrated that there were at least 13,177 persons here still in possession of their faculties. They were the no-shows at Neverfront . . . er, Frozenfront . . . er, Riverfront.

But why in the world would the other 46,302 come out in this? Steve Kreider, a wide receiver for the Bengals, out of Lehigh, pondered this and said, grinning: "It is a reflection on the failure of our educational system."

Prison Football:
Where Football Is Freedom

JANUARY 19, 1997

Puma's dream was so real that he woke up and tried to walk outside. And then he hit the bars and the steel door, and he rocked backward and it came to him—where he was, what he was.

A lifer. With no chance for parole. A convicted murderer. With 22 years served. And who knows how many more to go? Twenty? Thirty? Forty?

Ah, but a man doesn't dare let those kinds of thoughts in. They would drive him mad.

Puma says he didn't do it, didn't take a life, and he says that there is a man out there running loose who knows Puma is innocent and that, one day, conscience will force that man to come forward and they will open the doors and let Puma out into the sunlight.

And then you look into his eyes and see that he knows what his chances really are.

But Puma has one salvation. He has something to cling to. Football. It is his umbilical.

"When we're out there," he says, nodding out the window in the direction of a rutted, lumpy swath of clay pan, "we're not here anymore. We could be on the moon. The walls go away. Football is the ticket out. Well, for a couple of hours."

Puma is more than willing to share his salvation. He is the best athlete ever to perform inside the high, unforgiving walls of the State Correctional Institution at Graterford, a maximum-security prison, and he is the founder and commissioner of the prison's football league, which is now 10 years old. It is a seven-team league founded by inmates, run for inmates, run by inmates, with games officiated by inmates.

It's almost impossible to get away with anything.

"You can't con a con," says Raynard Gregory, the chief of officials, who is doing 30 to 60 for robbery. "We've heard it all."

Next Sunday—Super Bowl Sunday—will feature a doubleheader at Graterford, with an eight a.m. game between Demolition and the Blackstone Rangers, then a one p.m. game between the Steelers and the Raiders. That night, for the Super Bowl itself, it will be standing room only around the televisions scattered throughout the cell blocks. The betting—illegal, of course—will be office-pool heavy. But the currency will be cigarettes and chicken.

Chicken?

"Chicken is gold in here," Gregory says. "You got chicken, you can have whatever you want."

Puma likes the Packers.

Gregory smiles slowly, tightly, like a man with inside information.

"New England," he says, as though there can be no argument.

Gregory will watch the zebras, critique every call. Puma will watch Brett Favre and Drew Bledsoe. And let himself be tortured by one thought: That could have been me.

His real name is Alan Presbury. He is Inmate AF 5026. He is 44 years old, five feet 11, 210 pounds, most of it unyielding. Puma speaks to his speed. He is from North Philadelphia, the Strawberry Mansion section, and he was a legend on the streets and at the playgrounds. And then came the conviction and the sentence, and then he became the legend of Grater-ford. He has spent half his life behind its walls.

He could catch and pitch and play third. Not simultaneously. But close.

"Yankees . . . Braves . . . Pirates," he says, ticking off the major-league teams that wanted him, that he says tried to get him transferred and out on work release. But nothing ever came of it.

How long ago was that?

He looks at the ceiling and does what a man does best behind walls. He counts.

"Thirteen years," he says.

But it was as a quarterback that Puma became the talk of the cell blocks. His favorite receiver was Raynard Gregory.

"We were," Gregory says, "Montana and Rice."

Graterford used to play semipro teams from the Philadelphia area, but in 1985, there was a fight in the yard—a big, ugly one—and prison officials closed down the team.

Puma started up the rough-touch league. It's full contact. Mostly it's tackle, but without pads and helmets. By the fourth quarter, almost everyone is limping. The season is 22 weeks, November through March.

There are eight to a side. Everyone except the center is an eligible receiver. No chop blocks. Touching must be done with both hands. At the same time. This, of course, results in an argument on almost every play.

"I'm the most hated man in this institution," Gregory says proudly. "They know, if they didn't have us, there'd be fights all the time. And then the guards would get involved and we'd end up losing our football."

His face tells you that in a place where bad things happen, this would be the worst.

This is how much football means to them: "You'll have guys getting called to the visitors' center during a game," Puma says, "and they'll keep on playing. It's like when you were a kid and your mom would call you for dinner. 'One more play, Mom. One more quarter, Mom.' These guys got visitors and they want one more play, one more series. That's how much it means to them."

More than even family?

"Uh-huh."

The inmate population at Graterford is 4,000. Like a small college.

"I'd say the talent level is about Division II," Puma says. "We got some good athletes in here. There's a guy named Steinburg. He's got an arm. And sprinter's speed, too."

There is a lot of player turnover, and it has nothing to do with trades or free agency.

"Guys won't show up for a game," Puma says, "and you know they're in the Hole. Some of them go there and they get used to it. I don't think they want to come out. It's like they'll get in trouble on purpose so they can go back."

The football field at Graterford is a soupy bog when it rains and hard as an interstate in the winter. What grass there is grows in the end zone. But to Puma and Raynard and the rest of them, it is quite literally a field of dreams. The walls, the locks, the bars, the chains all fall away. There, they run free.

"It's what keeps me from going batty," Puma says.

But a man still thinks of the outside, doesn't he?

"First thing when you wake up," he says, "and last thing at night."

5

Horse Racing . . . Running Holes in the Wind

Smarty Jones at the Preakness: A Smarty Party

MAY 16, 2004

He rumbled down the stretch like rolling thunder, running on air and running all alone, the others already having abjectly surrendered, thoroughly cowed by this mighty machine, and the only remaining question was how much would he win by. The answer was as jaw-droppingly stunning as the performance itself—$11^1/_2$ lengths. No one in the previous 128 years of the Preakness had won with such ease and so convincingly.

And so on a sun-streaked, sticky day in mid-May, on a Pimlico track manicured and groomed for speed, with nine opponents each itching to take a shot at him, Smarty Jones, the newly minted Philadelphia folk hero, was asked to come back on only two weeks' rest and win another Triple Crown race.

He responded by obliterating the field.

It was a shattering, demoralizing defeat for the other colts, who are impressive in their own right, and it was a victory so smashing by Smarty that it invites favorable comparisons of the gutty little speedball to the glorious deeds of the great monster horse, Secretariat.

Smarty's overpowering triumph was the exclamation point on a giddy sports day in Philadelphia, with the Flyers beating Tampa Bay to pull even in the National Hockey League Eastern Conference finals at two games apiece about half an hour before Smarty went into the starting gate. The Phillies, who are on a road-trip rampage, chimed in with a 16-5 pounding of Colorado. Surely the World Series can't be far behind.

In Smarty, the city now has a double champion—Kentucky Derby and Preakness. The Belmont, that long and torturous final Triple Crown race, remains. Frankly, Smarty might win that one by three city blocks. If he has the lead in the stretch, it's all over.

Three weeks from now, the city could have both a Triple Crown winner and a Stanley Cup champion. Suddenly, after decades of despair and frustration, we are awash in delicious possibility. At the end of the victory parade, perhaps Smarty could eat oats from the Cup.

What he did yesterday was so astonishing as to beg hyperbole. Already ragingly popular in Philly, he has become the people's horse all over the country. The Preakness draws around 100,000, give or take, most years.

Yesterday, 112,668, far and away an attendance record, showed up at Pimlico, there to get sunburned, lubricated, and cheer madly for the little horse whose story keeps getting better every day.

On Smarty's race alone, the people at Pimlico poured $58,791,406 in wagers through the pari-mutuel windows. Yet another record. The public not only has handed over its heart to Smarty, but its wallet as well. Hard to tell which is the greater compliment.

At one point, he was bet down to 1-5.

You thought: The Philly contingent has shown up and they are betting on their guy with both hands.

From whatever perspective his portfolio is measured, Smarty Jones is impeccable. He has now won all eight races in which he has been entered. At eight different distances. At five different tracks. In five different states. He has beaten 77 horses.

Not only has no one beaten him, no one has passed him.

He is dominating, intimidating, relentless. His versatility seems limitless—run short, run long, run medium, run them all into the ground. And there is every reason to believe that he still has not run his best race.

"He's push-button now," said Smarty's jockey, the flinty, little Stewart Elliott.

"I had plenty of horse left at the end."

The other riders let you know with their testimony just what we have here.

"We may have seen history today," said Gary Stevens, who rode the second-place finisher, Rock Hard Ten. "I was no match for him. When I asked my guy for another gear, Smarty Jones had four gears left."

And Mike Smith, the rider on the front-running Lion Heart who was drilled into defeat and exhaustion by Smarty, said: "Me and Gary are on some great horses. The problem is, they were just born the same year as Smarty."

The win was something of a redemption for Elliott, whose last few days have been clouded by dredgings from his past involving alcohol and violence. But he said he would have no problem concentrating on the race, and obviously he didn't. Elliott made the right tactical move, and the only one he needed to make, by stalking Lion Heart and tucking inside when Lion Heart went wide on a turn. And then, with three-quarters of a mile run, Elliott leaned over and whispered in one twitching ear: "Let's go, Big Boy."

Smarty shot away. The others went down like the sun.

That Smarty had such acceleration was a confirmation and vindication for trainer John Servis, who refused to submit Smarty to a full workout in the interim between the Derby and the Preakness. Servis believed he had a fit colt and that to work him hard would be to needlessly use him up. The last week, the colt could barely be contained, so badly did he want to run.

Elliott gave him a trip without incident, and as a sign of Smarty's maturation, the once-skittish colt stood patiently in the starting gate for roughly five minutes while track handlers struggled to load the recalcitrant Rock Hard Ten, who threw Stevens.

"He [Smarty] is just unbelievable, and he just keeps getting better, the son of a gun," said Elliott.

The doubters had all their questions before the race: How will he run on a dry, fast track after winning the Derby in the slop? How will he react when he gets trapped in traffic, when he faces some adversity? Are five races in three months too tough a campaign? Isn't he overdue for a clunker?

It turns out all the questions were so much wishful thinking.

Smarty becomes the 29th horse to win the first two legs of the Triple Crown. But only 11 have gone on to win the Belmont. On June 5, it will be an even dozen.

What we have on our hands is a Super Horse.

Smarty Jones at the Belmont: He Never Stopped Running

JUNE 6, 2004

At the top of the stretch, he was in front by four lengths and you were sure the Triple Crown was his. After all, he had never, ever allowed another horse to pass him, this fierce and valiant little tiger.

But on this day, they had pack-hounded him all the way around the track, jackals nipping at wounded prey, pressuring and pestering. They had pressed him from the inside and from the outside, they had forced him three-wide early, and they had never permitted him to settle into a comfortable rhythm. Every breath, every stride was contested.

Still, he would hang on, wouldn't he? He would run his guts out and he would win anyway, wouldn't he? The racing gods wouldn't be this cruel, would they?

Fifty yards from the finish, the late-running Birdstone, a 36-to-1 shot who had hidden in the shadows, did the unthinkable. He overtook Smarty Jones, surged past him with powerful, ground-gulping strides. He won the Belmont Stakes. He left the splinters of shattered dreams scattered all over Belmont Park. He ruined the Smarty Party.

Afterward, the jockey, the trainer and the owners of Birdstone, stunned by what they had done, took turns saying the same thing over and over and over: "We're sorry, we're sorry, we're sorry."

Their apologies were heartfelt. As horse people, they realize how much Smarty Jones had done for their sport, how he had galvanized the country, how this had become a love story.

Now will come the howling cynics and the sneering skeptics to tell you that this was just another Philadelphia story, the kind that always seems to end badly. They will dredge up the Phillies of '64. And a certain World Series home run in '93. And any or all of the last three Eagles seasons.

But no, they are wrong. There is no curse over Philadelphia athletes and Philadelphia teams. No hex.

Smarty Jones lost to a horse that, on this particular day, was better. It happens. Often.

"It hurts to say it, but that's what makes this sport great," said John Servis, Smarty's trainer, a gracious loser and a class act.

"We tried our hardest," said Smarty's jockey, Stewart Elliott, as if apologizing for something that needed no apology.

Of course they had tried their hardest. He had pumped the reins furiously, he had shown Smarty the whip, shaking it, and in those last desperate lunges toward the finish he had flipped at the bridle, trying anything to muster one final burst.

And Smarty Jones dug in gamely, but for the first time in his nine-race career, he looked to his right and saw another horse going past, and there was nothing he could do about it. You wondered if that surprised him as much as it did the rest of us.

In the press box, where it is supposed to be silent as a tomb and where cheering is strictly prohibited, dozens of jaded adults watched Birdstone go past Smarty Jones and as they realized what was about to happen, they began to moan: "No . . . no . . . oh, no. . . ." It was a pitiful, passionate attempt to deny what we were seeing, to somehow prevent it, hold it back.

A horse does strange things to people. Many of them wonderful.

"He never stopped running," Elliott said. "We just couldn't . . . ."

He didn't finish the sentence. It wasn't necessary. They just couldn't hold off the other horse, that's all. And on this day, on a fast track cooked to accommodate speed, they may have found the bottom of Smarty Jones' well. Servis had always marveled at how Smarty always seemed to have something left. Servis said that the bottom would be reached on the day that Smarty lost.

The demanding distance of the Belmont—that devilish, sadistic mile and a half—has done in Triple Crown contenders before. It might have been a couple of city blocks too far for Smarty. That he couldn't hold on to that four-length lead strongly suggests as much.

Birdstone was bred for distance.

"He just wants to keep running," said Nick Zito, his trainer and a Belmont winner after five previous second-place finishes.

"I still think Smarty Jones will go down in history as a great horse," Zito added.

Certainly he will always have a place in Belmont's heart. The largest crowd in the 136 runnings of the Belmont Stakes showed up under glowering, occasionally leaky skies: 120,139. They came to see Little Red.

In all, around the country, more money was wagered on Smarty Jones than on any horse in history. Little Red captured and captivated the public. It was reported that one man had bought 6,000 two–dollar win tickets on Smarty, which he planned to hand out as souvenirs. I'll bet there will still be takers.

And so ends a glorious campaign, one that is not a failure at all. The horse won the Kentucky Derby, after all.

"That was our championship," Servis said.

And then he won the Preakness, and then on the first Saturday in June he came agonizingly close to the Triple Crown.

"Somebody said winning the Derby is like climbing Mount Everest," John Servis said. "We climbed it twice and tried to climb it too fast the third time. I don't think we have to hang our heads."

No. No, they don't.

It was left to Marylou Whitney, the owner of Birdstone, to put this in perspective: "Smarty Jones let people say, 'Hey, this could happen to me.'"

He gave hope.

Not a bad legacy.

They Win Our Hearts:
Chance of a Lifetime

MAY 4, 2007

In the shadow-streaked splendor of the first Saturday in May, edging toward twilight's last gleaming, they wait in the gate, snorting like steam engines, dancing impatiently on those matchstick legs, quivering with pent-up energy, muscles bunching and coiling, yearning to be unleashed.

Then the starter sets them free. They come boiling out in bumping, jumbling, altogether glorious chaos, and the drumbeat of their hooves sounds like rolling thunder. And one mile and one quarter later, in no more than two minutes, give or take a blink or two, one of them will have run the fastest of all through that shattering wall of noise down the homestretch, and the little man on the big horse's back will stand up in the stirrups in triumph and lean over and whisper into one of those twitching velvet ears: "You've won it, baby!"

In the winner's circle they will drape a blanket of red roses across those muscular shoulders, and all will smile for the camera. There are richer races. There are longer races. But there are none as famous as this one.

"When people find out what you do," said the jockey Jerry Bailey, "they always ask if you ever won the Kentucky Derby."

Bailey has, and more than most he realizes that the odds against it are discouragingly staggering. For starters, there is only one opportunity per animal per lifetime: the Derby is limited to those three years old—no younger, no older.

In 2004 in the U.S. of A., 34,642 thoroughbreds were foaled. Of those, 450 were nominated for the Triple Crown races—Derby, Preakness, Belmont. Tomorrow, for the 133rd running, the field will have been winnowed to fewer than two dozen. Even for a sport that gave us the term long shot, these are daunting odds.

In the words of the balladeer Dan Fogelberg: "The chance of a lifetime in a lifetime of chance."

There are no guarantees. The irony is that these magnificent creatures, half a ton and capable of 40 miles an hour, are also fragile, vulnerable, and sometimes easily spooked, given to jumping over shadows. One misstep . . .

Last year, a two-year-old named The Green Monkey was purchased for $16 million. Nagged by injury, it has yet to run a race. And might never.

For the last three years, the trainer of the year has been Todd Pletcher. He has saddled 14 mounts in Kentucky Derbies. He hasn't won one yet. In this year's Derby, he sends five to the post. We haven't always had the best horse, he said. And even when you do have the best horse, it doesn't always win.

Last year, the Derby was won powerfully, impressively, by a four-legged machine named Barbaro, who almost instantly won a huge following among the public. That following swelled two weeks later when, only a few strides into the Preakness, the colt's right hind leg seemed to come apart in a hideous explosion. There followed more than half a year of frantic attempts to, first, heal Barbaro, and finally, to save him. In the end, neither was possible.

The public outpouring was overwhelming. The colt's every hiccup was chronicled and analyzed. Clearly, Barbaro had tapped into an emotional hole.

The scoffers and hard-hearted ridiculed the mourners, sneered at such maudlin displays. It's a horse.

But, of course, he was much more than that. They all are. The sentimentalists among us are touched by their majesty, their nobility. We respond instinctively to their beauty, the liquid eyes, the nostrils working like a blacksmith's bellows. To stand next to one is to be awed by the power and the grace.

We don't always do well by them. Some of the medication is questionable at best. The racing surfaces ought to be safer, have some forgiving yield to them. The Triple Crown races should be spaced farther apart.

Once, a long time ago, it was called the Sport of Kings. The track was where you went to gamble. Then came the lotteries. Followed by the casinos. Tracks withered and turned into malls.

Now, the circle seems to come full—the trend is to "racinos." Slot machines stuffed into tracks, with some of the money funneled into larger purses, the intent alleged to be improved racing. Will it be the salvation of a sport? Or just a distraction?

There is a definition worth remembering—horse sense: the sense horses have not to bet on humans.

Secretariat: Big Red

SEPTEMBER 1989

He was the color of burnished copper, and he could race a hole through the wind. The public took to him as though he were a two-legged superstar, buying up pari–mutuel tickets on him that they preferred to keep and cherish rather than cash, and then visiting him in his retirement by the busload.

Yesterday, at age 19, on the Claiborne Farm in Paris, Kentucky that had been his lifelong home, Secretariat, heralded by many thoroughbred aficionados as the perfect racing machine, was put to sleep. He suffered from complications of a lethal hoof disease known as laminitis.

Secretariat's condition, which was diagnosed on Labor Day, "rapidly worsened" on Tuesday, said Gus Koch, assistant manager at Claiborne, putting the stallion in "extreme pain for the first time."

"When the inflammation occurs, swelling results," Koch said. "And since there is little room for swelling, this is a very painful condition."

Secretariat was put down by injection yesterday morning and buried on the Claiborne Farm in an oak casket lined with orange silk, the color used by Claiborne's racing stables.

He was fondly called "Big Red," for the shimmering chestnut sheen of his coat. Large and muscular, with an enormous stride, Secretariat was entered in 21 races, won 16 of them, and was retired in November 1973. He was only three years old at the time, but already had been syndicated for a then-record $6 million.

His reputation was established, embellished and then made into mythic proportions all in the space of six weeks in the spring of 1973. That was when he won the Triple Crown—the Kentucky Derby, in a record time that still stands; the Preakness, in which he surged from last to the lead as though he were toying with the field; and the Belmont, in which he set another record that remains and in which his margin of victory was a shattering 31 lengths.

Of all the Triple Crown championships, and there have been 11 of them, Secretariat's, the first Triple Crown in 25 years, is regarded as the most impressive, because he didn't just win, he destroyed the competition. And in the process he did for his sport what Babe Ruth did for his and Arnold Palmer for his—broadened its appeal, won over fans who didn't know a furlong from a fetlock but who loved to watch that big horse run, as if the race track was a current of air under him.

He had a distinctive stride, the muscles bunching in knots of power, his long legs reaching out in a ground-gulping gait. His stride once was measured at 25 feet. The conformation of his body was considered the anatomical ideal.

"He was the boss hoss, and he knew it. And so did everyone else," said Bobby Anderson, who was Secretariat's groom for more than six years at Claiborne.

There, on wide, emerald swatches of grass, Secretariat stood at stud, commanding $40,000 for each mating service and another $40,000 at conception. But for all his prowess on the track, he was something of a bust as a sire.

"A lot of people thought he would just go in the breeding shed and produce a whole string of little Secretariats," said Seth Hancock, the president of Claiborne. "But this business just doesn't work that way. The public probably was disappointed he didn't sire a colt as good as he was."

The closest that Secretariat came to reproducing himself was a colt named Risen Star, a muscular dark bay whose greatest triumph was winning the 1988 Belmont by $14^1/_2$ lengths, in a time second only to his daddy's. Secretariat also sired such stakes winners as Lady's Secret, General Assembly, Pancho Villa and Image of Greatness.

His greatest strength was in siring fillies who became successful broodmares. Six Crowns, for one, was the dam of Chief's Crown.

"He made a great broodmare sire," Hancock said, "and that ensured his place in sire history."

His place in racing history is unassailably secure.

Before Secretariat had even run in the 1973 Kentucky Derby, Hancock, then a young man trying to establish his own reputation, already had persuaded investors to buy up shares, at considerable cost, in the syndication of the colt. Hancock's future hung on Secretariat's performance.

"Rumors were flying all over the track before the Derby," Hancock remembered. "They said Red was broke down, couldn't run a mile and a quarter. So then he went out and ran the record," one minute, 59 and two–fifths seconds.

"And then he backed up that Derby with his Preakness, and I can still see him in that first turn, when he went from last to first in just a sixteenth of a mile. It was pretty awesome.

"And then the Belmont, well, anyone who's ever gone to a sporting event would have to say that was one of the most incredible performances they've ever seen. You know, he ran 2:24 that day for the mile and a half, and he was going right into the teeth of a strong wind in the backstretch."

In retirement, Secretariat enjoyed a champion's popularity. Unfailingly, his birthday (March 30) would bring bags of mail and boxes of carrots and treats, including his favorite, peppermint candy.

"We get tour groups coming through here all the time," Anderson said. "Owners, breeders, horse fans, school kids, all kinds of people. But it doesn't matter what group it is, the first thing 99 percent of them want to know is, 'Where's Secretariat?' "

Spotting a camera, the horse would strike a regal pose. When visitors stopped by his $1^1/_2$-acre paddock, he would charge down the hill, snorting and bellowing.

"He loves it," said John Sosby, manager of Claiborne Farm. "It's 'Look at me, I'm the king.' If he could talk, he might be the type to brag a little."

"Tell you one thing," Anderson said. "He knew who he was, and there won't ever be another like him."

6

Hockey . . .
Keep Your Teeth
in Your Pockets

Gretzky:
The Great One

APRIL 19, 1999

He left us as he had come, with a quiet grace and an understated elegance, making a game of thunderous collisions between toothless and stitched men seem somehow more civilized simply by his presence and his genius.

Wayne Gretzky handled the hardest part of being a professional athlete there is—the goodbye—with a final-curtain performance that was as smooth as the ice on which for 21 years he embroidered his swooping circles and elaborate curicues while other skaters flopped foolishly in vain pursuit.

One of the longest-running and most mesmerizing shows in all of sport, The Great Gretzky, gave its 1,695th, and last, performance yesterday, an early-spring matinee not far from Broadway, in teary Madison Square Garden.

The rest of us cried, but he tried to shush away our sobs. He crinkled that pale and wan, jughandle-eared, hawk-nosed face into one of those lopsided grins and winked shyly and urged us to make this a celebration.

That simply was not possible.

For his leaving is a loss of a magnitude beyond measuring at the moment. While it is true that no player—not even Ruth or Jordan or Gretzky—is bigger than the game, the inescapable fact is that hockey was allowed to grow, to expand into cities in which it never even snows, because of Wayne Gretzky.

And now, as hockey falters, TV ratings barely a blip and interest waning, its biggest name leaves it even more diminished.

The greater loss for the rest of us is the example that he set, as sportsman and missionary and ambassador, as self-effacing gentleman and as star without an unchained ego.

He did score yesterday. But then, how could he have not, given his exquisite penchant for drama? It was an assist, number 1,963, another one of those passes from God threaded through unsuspecting defenders and onto the waiting stick of Brian Leetch for the easiest kind of goal.

It enabled the New York Rangers, the fourth NHL team for whom The Great One has played, to tie the Pittsburgh Penguins, 1-1, in the second period. It seemed only fitting that the game then went into overtime, almost as though even the hockey gods themselves were reluctant to release him. The Penguins eventually won, 2-1, the goal scored by Jaromir Jagr, who hadn't planned to play the final game of the season until he found out that it would be Gretzky's last.

After he scored, Jagr embraced Gretzky and kissed his cheek, and then Gretzky, bent over in fatigue, skated away. He looked drawn, his face strained. He looked older than 38, and you could understand why.

He did a curtain call, a spotlight skate. And then another. He had his teammates come out. He skated a final farewell lap, reaching out to touch the hands of several children.

The entire game was played to the emotional accompaniment of sticks clattering against the boards and drumming on the ice, the players' time-honored ritual paying tribute to one of their own.

"This is the right time. In my heart, I know this is the right decision," he repeated when asked about his retirement.

And because he was at peace with that decision, he was able to make it through such an emotionally wrenching day mostly dry-eyed. He was finally overwhelmed during a center-ice team photo and had to swallow his own tears.

Gretzky was, he recalled, all of nine years old when a Canadian sportswriter hung on him the most impossible of nicknames—The Great One.

"The pressure and the name just stuck ever since," he said. It was the first time you ever remember hearing him even faintly allude to the unfairness of what we expected from him, and then came to take for granted.

The National Hockey League is all too aware of the size of the crater he leaves behind. And in an unprecedented move, the league announced just before face-off yesterday that number 99 is to be forever banned from all jerseys. Gretzky thus joins Jackie Robinson as the only athletes whose numbers have been retired not only by their teams, but by an entire sport.

Perhaps the best perspective I can give you from which to view him is this: In our business we have hanging from our necks assorted bits of plastic and pasteboard that serve as media credentials, passports into locker rooms and dugouts that we take for granted and that "civilians" would kill for. Usually, we discard these IDs on our way to the next airport and the next town and the next stadium.

But some, a very few, we keep. Roses from a special dance. Like the one from the night Henry Aaron smote the home run that passed Ruth. Like those from Olympics. And the Masters.

Wayne Gretzky's last game belongs in that memories category. The Rangers knew it, knew we would drop our mask of feigned indifference and elaborate nonchalance for this performance. So the credentials they passed out are laminated and come attached to a sturdy cord rather than the usual kite string. On the front is a color photo of Gretzky, back turned and left glove aloft as he skates away.

"It seemed like it went by too fast," Janet Gretzky said yesterday.

She didn't want him to retire. She wanted him to play one more year, have one season of collecting tribute. But he had no such interest in an extended and contrived goodbye tour.

"I thought maybe it would make him happier," his wife said, "but now I don't think so."

The commissioner of the NHL, Gary Bettman, had tried to talk Wayne Gretzky into one more year, but he had declined, politely but firmly, and good for him. He had too much respect for the game and no interest at all in an 82-game sideshow, with face-offs delayed and the flow of each game interrupted.

And more than that, Wayne Gretzky has no pathetic, craving need to look up night after night, in arena after arena, and see video highlights of how great he was.

He doesn't need to be reminded.

He knows, he knows.

Flyers Playoff:
The Blade Runners

APRIL 28, 2008

Outside, a late April rain, cold and unforgiving, is slashing at the night. Inside, the Blade Runners are busily at it, mucking and checking and grinding and otherwise forcefully demonstrating why those who play hockey keep their teeth in their pants pockets.

The Montreal Canadiens, who are pretty sure they invented the game and don't mind reminding you of that, and the Philadelphia Flyers, who are still pursuing that long and winding quest to recapture their glory days, are about to resume their playoff hostilities.

But first, through the digital magic of however it is they do this, the Flyers present, from the archives, their talisman for all these years, Kate Smith. She performs a duet with the current resident good luck charm, Lauren Hart, who has, as they say in the business, a great set of pipes. The two do "God Bless America" so sweet and pure that, as always, it raises the hackles on the nape of your neck.

And that, folks, is quite enough with the civility, for this is hockey, after all, and we've already wastefully let three minutes go by without thumping someone.

It was anticipated that the first glove dropping would be, oh, say, three seconds after the puck dropped, because the two teams, in just two games, had managed to say snippy things about each other and set the blood to boiling. And yet the game is almost 18 minutes in before the first flare goes off. The Flyers' Steve Downie swoops in on Montreal goalie Carey Price, who has strayed from the crease and is all alone in the open, a deer halfway across the interstate.

Goalies are not fair game, no matter how far they roam. But Downie cannot resist. He aims for the goalie's legs and, using his stick like an oversized spatula, he flips Price. The Canadiens take outraged exception and the Flyers must retaliate, of course, so soon the ice is littered with gloves and sticks, and unkind things are being said about ancestry. The population of the penalty box goes up by four.

The first period ends with no score, because Price has been a bit shaky but still undented, and because the Flyers' Martin Biron has been impregnable. He sprawls, he smothers, he snatches bullets with his glove hand.

The Canadiens have that fuzzy, puzzled look that asks: "How'd he stop that one?"

The Flyers finally score in the second period when Scottie Upshall, who has stayed on the ice beyond his shift in order to get in one more rush, steams in on Price, has the time to tee up the puck, and fires something that trails blue flame. Price never sees it, and the netting behind him billows. Upshall's risk to stay for one more rush is richly rewarded.

Price seems flummoxed, and his bewilderment only intensifies moments later when Mike Richards curls across the middle and, through a screen, rips a cannon shot that ricochets off Price's glove, then off a post. That sort of stuff—off the post, off the other post, off the Zamboni, off Billy Penn's hat—happens a lot, you may have noticed.

Now the Flyers have a 2-0 lead, but this is not the cause for raucous celebration you might think. Because during these playoffs, the Flyers have treated a two-goal lead like something on the bottom of their shoe…er, skates.

Ah, but not tonight. No, 2-0 quickly, briskly, becomes 3-0 when R.J. Umberger fires home a rebound that leaves Price sprawled face down in frustration. In a 13-minute span, the Flyers have scored three times. More impressive, they have scored twice in the last three minutes of the second period.

Now it is most definitely the Flyers' game to lose. Having already eliminated one team that was seeded higher than they (Washington), they are positioned to seize a 2-1 lead over another team rated above them.

All that is required over the next 20 minutes is to keep the heat off Biron and defend fiercely. Easy enough to say, but the opponent is prideful and resolute.

That task becomes that much more difficult when defenseman Derian Hatcher collects a costly, and considering the circumstances, utterly thoughtless, five-minute boarding penalty, plus a game misconduct. Sure enough, the Canadiens cash in on that power play, poking around in front of Biron like clam–diggers, finally nudging the puck in.

And mere moments later, the price on Hatcher's penalty doubles—another Montreal power play goal. More than half of the third period is yet to be played and what had been a romp has become a noose-tightener.

It gets even tighter when the Flyers present yet another gift to the Canadiens, another power play at the worst possible moment, this one against defenseman Lasse Kukkonen. But they manage to kill that one, and Biron is heroic in the turning away.

The Flyers get their own break—Montreal, so desperate and so anxious to mount a final charge, is caught with too many men on the ice.

Power play, Flyers. Ah, but they cannot convert the advantage. Of course not. Why would they want to take the comfortable way out when they are flourishing in adversity.

The game ends with the puck on a Montreal player's stick, the last shot unfired. So, that thread the Flyers were hanging by didn't unravel after all.

Right about now, an exhale is highly recommended.

Hextall:
The Man in the Mask

APRIL 13, 1995

He waits at the top of the right face-off circle, and one by one the other Flyers glide past him, touching gloved fists with him as they cruise by.

And then Eric Lindros skates to the goal and takes his stick in both hands and begins to swing it like a man trying to bring down a sequoia. He administers lusty two-handers to Ron Hextall, his own man.

Whomp . . . whomp . . . whomp . . . whomp . . . .

It sounds like muffled artillery. Eric Lindros digs in, pivoting for leverage, hacking away at his own goaltender, always to the thick padding on Hextall's left leg.

Whomp . . . whomp . . . whomp . . . whomp . . . .

Ron Hextall stands there impassively. Not so much as a blink. Like a man with a bulletproof vest accepting shotgun blasts.

Eight times Eric Lindros slashes his goalie's right leg, and then pats his knee once, twice, with his stick, nods in satisfaction and skates away, ready now for the National Anthems of Canada and the United States.

Now, and only now, are the Flyers officially ready to play hockey. The ritual of the ax is over.

Eric Lindros is sufficiently warmed up. Presumably so is Ron Hextall.

Sure enough, only 44 seconds in and the red light twinkles. Alas, it is the one above Hextall.

He looks shaky on the first two Montreal shots, fumbling for them, like a man feeling his way for furniture in a room with the lights out. And Pierre Turgeon alertly scavenges among the rubble of a five-player pile-up, sweeps away the puck that nobody else seems able to get to, and guns it past Hextall.

This is an important goal for the Canadiens. The proudest franchise in the sport is embarrassingly meek and mysteriously unsuccessful on the road this season—only three wins in alien rinks. And they have been bounced around by the Flyers this season, outscored, 17-6, in the first three games.

This is an important game for both teams. The truncated season has only 10 games left. Montreal is laboring just to make the playoffs, difficult as that is to believe, and the Flyers have a more ambitious goal. If they can win their division, which they lead, not only do they qualify for the postseason, but they are sure of home ice in the first two rounds.

So the Canadiens are trying to save face this night, and the Flyers are trying to tighten their grip around Montreal's windpipe. And we will see once again how the volatile Ron Hextall performs.

The suspicion is that the Flyers can go a long way this spring. The Cup could be stolen. They have one line that is, literally, unstoppable. Their defense improves, and Gary Desjardins grows on you by the minute.

So it comes down to goaltending. But then doesn't it always? A hot goalie can cover a lot of weaknesses. Conversely, a struggling goalie makes his own defense overanxious, makes his own offense start to press.

In his old age, Hextall has become more stand-up and also more erratic. But like a sinkerball pitcher, he believes that he plays better the more frequently he plays. If he is on the verge of exhaustion, he can be brilliant.

His effort is unflagging, as is his passion. For better or worse, the Flyers will finally go as far as he . . . well, you know the rest. If he is fumbling for the puck, as he is this night, the Flyers likely go out in the first round. If he is on, and sustains it for two months, well, the Flyers could make a serious run at a Cup you think is still a couple of seasons away.

The Flyers need less than three minutes to tie this game, Brent Fedyk digging the puck loose from against the boards, swooping behind the Montreal net and stuffing it past a startled Patrick Roy.

He is as good a goalie as there is in the league, and yet he always struggles against the Flyers, no matter if they are good or bad. It is one of the mysteries of the sport. In 16 games against Philadelphia, Roy has exactly one win. Frankly, you wonder why the Canadiens do not insert someone else between the pipes. How bad can it be?

But perhaps the Canadiens reason that this would be to admit defeat beforehand. And these are the Canadiens, after all. Haughty. Proud. They concede nothing.

The Flyers give up a short–handed goal, but this one is not all Hextall's fault. The Canadiens come at him with a two-on-one, and he gets tangled up with Desjardins.

The Flyers tie the game and then Fedyk, hooked, pinwheels into Roy, jolting him with a knee to the ear. Roy arises, after ministrations, and proceeds to make two brilliant saves.

At the other end, Ron Hextall sees only nine shots in two periods. He still looks unsteady, as though his calibrator, his range-finder, is a click slow.

But he steadies himself as the game wears on and is unyielding in the crucial closing minutes.

The Flyers win. Artistry is irrelevant—only the result matters.

Tim and Kathy Kerr:
Forever Ended Way Too Soon

OCTOBER 17, 1990

He was an oak, and she was a willow.

He plants himself in front of the net, tall and strong and unyielding, and defensemen pry and prod and poke at him. But that is like trying to uproot a stump that has been in the ground a long, long time. Tim Kerr will not be budged. They slash and whack at him—men with no teeth and mean intentions—but they cannot move him.

Naturally, then, when bulldozers are used in vain, when dynamite won't work, what is called for is a woman. Naturally, he was a sucker for her. Naturally, the oak who cannot be dislodged by the toothless muggers turned to helpless mush whenever he was around her. It is the way of the world.

Kathy Kerr was petite and sinewy, and Tim Kerr planned to spend forever with her. Except, abruptly, with no regard for anyone's wishes, forever has ended a lot sooner than either one of them planned.

Kathy Kerr, who had given birth to a daughter only days before, died yesterday morning. It makes no sense. But, then, tragedy hardly ever does.

What happened is one more wrenching reminder that, while life can be so very, very sweet for our sporting heroes, it also can be so very, very cruel.

From the outside, Tim Kerr would seem to have lucked into all that we envy. One day, he was a 17-year-old kid from Windsor, Ontario, just across the river from Detroit, making $18 a week playing junior hockey; and the next, he was a professional athlete, the Flyers' top gun, with a paycheck swollen with zeroes and commas, with a summer home at the shore and a speedboat, with idolaters craving his autograph, with worshipers craving to cater to his every whim.

What was not to like?

There was, of course, a price. There is always a price. And, usually, the greater the reward, the higher the price. Tim Kerr's bills took the form of shoulder surgery. Over and over, so many operations. They went into his shoulder so many times, it would have been more convenient just to put in a zipper, rather than stitches. And, always, there was the drudgery and the pain, and the boredom of rehabilitation.

And, always, there was his wife. For reassurance. For support. For comfort. Always, the oak had the willow.

Tim Kerr knew he was playing on borrowed time. His shoulder reminded him. So he was never as blinded by celebrity as some of them are.

Three summers ago, when the metal screw that had been put in after yet another operation came loose—they told him the reason was that his shoulders were too big!—he said: "This isn't something I'm happy about, but I'm not going to ruin my life over missing a couple of hockey games when all you have to do is look around a little bit to see what life is all about."

He showed a nice sense of balance, a nice perspective. And they lived it, too—the oak and the willow. They gave back.

Tim Kerr runs a hockey school every summer. He has organized an annual summer run in Avalon, New Jersey, that raises thousands for the blind. Kathy Kerr chaired the annual Flyers' Wives Fight for Lives Carnival last winter. It raised $760,000 to fight leukemia.

Yes, the oak and the willow had it together. They had each other. They had their dogs. They had a stepdaughter, and after Kathy Kerr suffered miscarriages, they adopted a little girl. And, as is so often the case, not long after they adopted, Kathy Kerr learned that she was pregnant.

When the Flyers opened their 1990-91 home season 10 days ago, the message board above center ice flashed congratulations to Tim and Kathy Kerr on the birth of their daughter, Kimberly.

The Flyers won. Their first goal was scored by Tim Kerr. On a rebound from right in front of the net.

Right where the oak always takes root. Now the oak has lost the willow.

In all that he has endured, Tim Kerr has adhered to the athlete's credo of striving for equilibrium.

"I don't get too high in good times," he said in an interview last winter, "and I don't get too low in bad times. Listen, if you're looking for real troubles, you don't have to look too far in this world."

When all of the tears have finally been cried, there will be one comfort for Tim Kerr in his agony, one source of solace, and that is that the willow has left behind for the oak a living reminder of herself and of what they had together.

7

Boxing . . .
Protect Yourself
at All Times

Ali at the Super Bowl:
Still the Greatest

FEBRUARY 6, 2000

Even from the back, you recognize him. His head is the giveaway. It bobs up and down, faster even than the thumping of his own stout heart. He is a prisoner of the palsy. It is the insidious part of the cruel disease that has enfolded him in its relentless embrace.

Once, as he let the world know in a self-indulgent catchphrase that was appealing despite its braggadocio, he could float like a butterfly, dancing uncatchably across a meadow. Now, Parkinson's disease locks his body into a brittle rigidity and creates uncontrollable tremors.

And yet he has never—publicly—bemoaned his lot.

As always, when you encounter him from time to time, you are struck by his dignity in the face of all this indignity.

When he does speak of it, he always says the same essential thing: "I am being reminded that I am just a man. Just like everyone else. I am learning. You can learn, too."

Learn what, exactly? How to confront our own mortality. How to cope with the inevitabilities that await us all, the aging, the onset of infirmity, the inescapable vulnerabilities.

Yes, all that. All that and one thing more: How to resist.

For Muhammad Ali has taken the poet's impassioned plea to heart. He rages. He rages against the dying of the light.

He surfaced at the Super Bowl last week. Unannounced and unexpected, he showed up in the makeshift media lounge shortly after sunset. The media headquarters hotel in Atlanta had arranged to pipe in the Mike Tyson–Julian Francis fight from Manchester, England.

And without warning, there he was. All in black. Moving in that slow, hesitant, determined shuffle. The holder of the best seat in the house, a black leather easy chair squarely in front of the big–screen TV, leaped to his feet. Ali accepted the gift with a nod, and sat slowly, heavily.

Word spread. Ali's here.

The room was jammed. Keep in the mind the nature of the crowd. Career cynics. Terminal hard cases. Skeptics of the first rank who are jaded by constant exposure to the legitimate legends and the counterfeit ones. And yet these, the eternally unimpressed, fell all over themselves, literally, trying to catch a glimpse of Ali.

Earlier in the week, three vaguely famous retirees—Wayne Gretzky, Michael Jordan and John Elway—had held a joint press conference to announce an e-commerce venture. The three together roused mild curiosity.

But Ali's presence very nearly brought down the house. Again, literally. He sat like Buddha, round and serene and contented.

He dipped his trembling fingers into a small cellophane bag and withdrew pretzels and chewed slowly, methodically. He sipped now and then from a plastic bottle of soda, his movements marked by an exaggerated deliberateness. It struck you that he fed himself like the very old feed themselves. Yet he is only 57.

Each time that you see him, you never fail to be stabbed with poignancy. Nor do you fail to feel admiration and a certain reassurance: He's still here.

A room full of hardened and frequently uncharitable hearts all watched him chewing, mesmerized. It was extraordinary. A man fed himself pretzels, and people gaped as though a spaceship had just set down and an alien was having himself a picnic.

What is most remarkable is that, as famous and as adored as he was when he was an active athlete, Muhammad Ali has become more famous, more revered, in retirement. His appeal does not diminish; it grows.

It is a phenomenon that happens to only a few—Joe DiMaggio and Ted Williams spring to mind—but never on the scale of Ali.

After only the first round of the fight, Ali got up slowly and walked out. He said not a word, but there was a twinkle in his eye. He was saying: I have seen more than enough. It occurred to you that it was just about the best-timed, silence-speaks-volumes exit you had ever seen.

People laughed in appreciation. Then they clapped. And they never clap.

Evander Holyfield, a gallant man, said: "Ali never was a dangerous fighter, but they learned to love him because he beat everybody. I beat everybody, too. I think they'll love me more when I'm gone."

His voice was wistful.

Ali began as a hustler. Now he is treated as a holy man. All he has to do is walk across an empty hotel lobby, and magically it is filled, and the people press toward him with an obvious reverence.

He was glib and daring and defiant. Now, he brushes crumbs from his swelling belly and frequently dozes in the middle of conversation. He awakens without apology. Not that any is needed.

There is a glow about him. He looks bemused. The inescapable impression is that he knows things, but is not always allowed to share them.

His voice is usually a whisper, raspy and thick. But he talks with his face, with his eyebrows, with the twinkle.

He has been, for almost half a century now, a symbol. Sometimes of defiance and daring. Sometimes of skill and wit. Sometimes of faith and conviction.

Now he has come to symbolize the courage of coping, the valor of unceasing resistance, the bravery of persistence.

The irony, it strikes you, is that it is no longer necessary for him to proclaim himself The Greatest.

We know. We know.

Drama Bahama:
Dance of Losers

DECEMBER 11, 1981

Paradise Island, Bahamas—It is being billed as "Drama in Bahama." It is more like "Trauma in Bahama."

So far, it has been a chaotic shambles, featuring late-night muggings, a shadowy promoter whose response to all questions is a glare, the threat by at least one of the combatants to refuse to enter the ring until he sees some front money, and the ever-popular local pastime known as Gouge-the-Tourist.

It is supposed to unfold here tonight, a 10-fight card showcased by yet another return of Muhammad Ali, who has finally surrendered in his futile Battle of the Bulge.

Ali arrived for the weigh-in yesterday 46 minutes late, which was about as prompt as anything else has been here all week. With much fanfare, the scales were brought in; they may have been as rigged as the prices on local menus.

He stepped on the scales; they groaned, he frowned. His weight was announced as $236^1/_2$. He shook his head and stepped off, stepped back on, glared at the weight mechanism. It was not intimidated and refused to budge.

It is the heaviest Ali has ever been for any fight by six pounds. Clearly, he is past the point where even starvation will melt off his considerable insulation.

"I wanted to be 235," he said, and then rationalized his blubber with this intriguing logic: "The extra weight will help me in the clinches."

If he fights as he has in recent years, there will be many more clinches and embraces than actual punching.

Ali's opponent is Trevor Berbick, whose weight (218) was not nearly as interesting as his demand for money. Berbick has heard the reports that this financial fiasco already has resulted in some of the participants having to take pay cuts. If the attendance is as low as expected, a lot of people are going to take a bath in red ink.

"I need some guarantees before I get in the ring," Berbick said.

James Cornelius, who is promoting this charade, stood by Berbick's elbow and shouted: "There ain't gonna be no problems."

Writers tried to press this point, and Cornelius, who has been either vague or just plain snappish, flared again.

"I came here for the weigh-in," he yelled. "No questions. If you want to ask something, ask about the damn fight."

Which is what we have been trying to do all week, only to have Cornelius duck behind a phalanx of local gendarmes and angrily instruct them: "Move those people back."

Cornelius identifies himself as president of Sports Internationale Ltd. One early press release described him as "a young enterprising businessman from Atlanta." Now he claims he is from Los Angeles, where he is in "private business." What kind of business? "No more questions," he said, taking refuge behind another squad of black leather militia.

The fight was originally scheduled for December 5th. The site, the Queen Elizabeth Sports Centre, was first claimed to have a capacity of 40,000. Now they are saying it will seat 17,000. There are reports that barely 5,000 tickets have been sold. Attempts to get a figure from Cornelius produce only veiled threats.

At least two different public relations outfits already have bailed out, one saying: "These people are in way over their heads. The best action is going to be all the litigation once this is over, assuming it ever takes place."

Patti Dreifuss, a competent, experienced media relations veteran of these boxing wars, is, by her own admission, close to being a basket case. Among other things, she was shown a map that indicated spaces for 204 members of the working press at ringside. When she visited the site, she found accommodations for only 40.

Phone communications to the states are a hopeless tangle, with interminable waits and fuzzy, virtually inaudible connections. Yet a representative of Batelco (Bahama Telephone Company) called a surprise meeting with the media and demanded a down payment of $100 for each ringside phone with "dedicated service." No credit cards accepted. Only 16 such phones are available. This same outfit, only a few days ago, had assured those who inquired that no deposits would be necessary.

As for Cornelius, he has been accused by Don King, the flamboyant promoter, of assault. King charges that Cornelius and four other men visited him in his hotel room in Freeport one night this week, ordered him to leave the country, and punctuated that order by beating him up. Cornelius, of course, has no comment.

There is a suspicion that whatever fistic action may have taken place in King's hotel room was livelier than will unfurl in the ring tonight. As closely as anyone is able to determine, of the 10 fighters involved in the five principal bouts, only two come in having won their last outing.

The undercard may be more entertaining than the main event. It includes heavyweights Greg Page against Scott LeDoux; Earnie Shavers (who underwent surgery for a detached retina) against Jeff Sims; the first fight for Thomas Hearns, now a junior welterweight, since his September loss to Sugar Ray Leonard (he fights Ernie Singletary); and light-heavyweight Eddie Mustafa Muhammad against Mike Hardin.

Finally, sometime around 10 p.m., Ali will fight for the 61st time since he turned professional way back in 1960. Assuming, of course, that Trevor Berbick's fiscal demands have been met or he is at least mollified enough to even show up.

The weigh-in was the usual confusion, about as organized as a cattle drive. But Ali, who has used these rituals before to talk trash, chose this time to employ a different sort of psychology. An acknowledged master actor in this Theater of the Absurd, Ali showed up this time wearing his best I-am-serious face. There was no rolling-eyed ranting; he spoke in a voice that was almost a whisper.

"It's important that I be 100 percent serious for this," he said. "No clowning, no rope-a-dope, no Ali-shuffle, no making faces. There is no time for that now. This is too serious. I have too many critics to make eat their words."

Ringside seats are selling for $1,000 apiece. Sales obviously are slow, as evidenced by the announcement that special $10 tickets were now on sale.

Presumably, binoculars are not included. From those seats, the action in the ring will be only a rumor.

Drama in Bahama? Hardly. More like Night of the Losers.

A Fat Chance
in Paradise

DECEMBER 10, 1981

Paradise Island, Bahamas—To describe Muhammad Ali as merely fat and 40 is not totally accurate. He will not, after all, turn 40 until next month. As for the weight, well, he tries to camouflage that with bulky, loose-fitting sweatsuits. They may have come off the rack of the nearest maternity shop.

His camp followers insist he is down to 232. It is suspect by at least 10 pounds. Layers of loose suet hang in folds around his waist, jiggling. There should be no way that his opponent in this, yet another sequel of Ali Returns, could miss such an ample target as Ali's blubbery midsection. Nonetheless, Angelo Dundee has brought out of retirement a huge protective harness that Ali last used when he fought George Chuvalo, the Canadian roughneck. It is an immense, girdle-like belt with an oversized cup, armor plating for Ali's groin.

His opponent here tomorrow night, Trevor Berbick, like Chuvalo, is rumored to land several punches in that exquisitely painful area of the human anatomy referred to diplomatically as "south of the border."

Berbick is a Jamaican who migrated northward to become heavyweight champion of Canada, and, with his awkward style, forced Larry Holmes to go the limit, 15 frustrating rounds. That a defeat is his most notable claim to distinction tells you all you need to know about Berbick.

Chuvalo, now retired, has said of Berbick: "I could beat him six weeks after I'm dead."

Despite such contemptuous judgment, there is considerable opinion that Berbick will handle Ali, and not with all that much difficulty. Just as the foundation of a house irretrievably settles with age, Ali's frame has gone soft. There is also the worry his plumbing has suffered; kidney damage, they whisper.

There are a thousand theories about why he is attempting yet another comeback, especially since the most recent one, 15 months ago against Holmes, was such an abject failure. His corner ran up the white flag after 10 rounds.

Ali, slumped on his stool, face puffed, had not won a round.

Vanity, pride, ego . . . they all goad him on. But the most urgent driving force may be a financial one. Ali needs the money, even though he will pocket barely over one million dollars for this one, far short of what he is used to commanding.

It numbs the mind to reflect that here we have the greatest money-making athlete in history, and he has a cash-flow problem. He has won, in boxing purses alone, close to $70 million. Herculean profligacy and incredibly inept money management are required to go through that kind of money.

But Ali has expensive tastes. He has had some bad investments. Most of all, he may be the all-time soft touch. He has heard every contrived hard-luck story that ever came down the pike, and still he succumbs to many of them. Part of that is out of generosity; part of it is because, when he is not champion, he still needs adoration and if it must be bought, he will pay. This is not to suggest that he is destitute. There is still his Deer Lake training compound up in the Pennsylvania mountains, a prime piece of real estate. And there is his palatial mansion in Los Angeles, for which he paid $1.5 million and spent another million furnishing.

But there is this gnawing feeling that one day all his holdings may be auctioned off. Though he has vowed he will be the exception, you have this sad premonition that one day he will wind up like the late Joe Louis, busted and out on the streets.

Ali's concerns now, however, are only of a short-range nature.

"Six months from today," he was saying, "I will again be champion. Mike Weaver has challenged the winner of this fight. I will beat Weaver, become champion for the fourth time, and at the age of 40. Then I will retire."

He paused, then, as is his habit, hedged.

"Of course, I'll have to see what happens between Gerry Cooney and Holmes."

His spiel is unchanged, a monologue of fractured poetry and hyperbole, of bold predictions and outrageous challenges, of boastful comparisons between himself and Christopher Columbus or the Wright Brothers. ("We are the same because we have unlimited vision; we can see farther than others.") It is the same old show, but he has found a new audience. The Bahamas is virgin territory for Ali. They, of course, lap it up. He, in turn, feeds them what they want to hear.

"I had to come to a black country to get a license to fight again," he says.

He does not add that is because everyone else has a conscience.

George Foreman:
Holding Back the Night

NOVEMBER 7, 1994

He was doing exactly what an old man is supposed to do when he fights a young man. He was losing and he was bleeding, and you were hoping they would stop it.

And then George Foreman found Michael Moorer's chin with a nuclear-tipped straight right hand late on Saturday night, and everything in sports and in life was turned gloriously inside out and wonderfully upside down.

A 45-year-old man is heavyweight champion of the world, and you grope for something to compare it with, and you come up empty, because there isn't anything.

No one this old has ever done the equal of this. Oh, Jack Nicklaus won golf tournaments and Nolan Ryan threw no-hitters. But golf balls and baseballs don't hit back.

More than anything else, though, this is a feel-good story.

Sports has treated us shabbily of late. Seasons are truncated or aborted. Owners and players are equally consumed with greed. Disenchantment is with us. Our games leave us unfulfilled, dissatisfied.

And comes now this bald old fat man who has remade himself, who has metamorphosed from a sullen, despicable bully into an engaging geezer who sells street-corner dreams and now has made them seem attainable.

You look at George Foreman, at that broad, pleasant face that is perpetually wreathed in a patronly smile; you listen to him make gentle, self-deprecating jokes about his age and his diet, and you can feel the corners of your mouth begin to curl upward.

George Foreman gives us reason to smile, and it has been a long time since any of our mercenaries did that for us.

In his first incarnation 21 years ago, he took the heavyweight title from Joe Frazier with a ferocious two-round, six-knockdown annihilation; 20 years ago, he lost the title to Muhammad Ali.

Today, Joe Frazier climbs through the ring ropes on fight nights and bathes in the celebrity-introduction applause, and then disappears. Today,

Muhammad Ali shuffles and slurs his way through life, and it makes you weep to see the frozen smile, the palsy. And today, when he could just as easily be bloated and wasted and dissipated, an old man with broken dreams for companions, George Foreman is none of those things.

Instead, he is once again heavyweight champion of the world.

He had to go to court and sue to win the right to fight for the title. The cynics, with reason, feared this was more burlesque than boxing. There was also legitimate concern that a 45-year-old man could be seriously hurt being punched by a muscular, mean opponent 19 years his junior.

The physicians on the Nevada Athletic Commission insisted on extra tests before they would agree to sanction the fight, and when they were done probing George Foreman, they shook their heads in wonder.

He is some specimen, the cardiologist said, awed. He has a child's retinas, the ophthalmologist marveled. George Foreman is, they concluded, a freak of nature.

Maybe he is, maybe he isn't. But there is some sweet wellspring within him that he tapped on Saturday night.

With his face swelling and with blood leaking from a cut on his cheekbone, with his legs unsteady beneath him, and with all the judges' cards showing he was hopelessly behind, George Foreman had only one desperate chance to win.

He needed a knockout.

And late in the 10th round, Moorer relaxed his guard, for no more than an eyeblink really, and George Foreman rushed a locomotive of a left jab through that opening and followed with that thunderclap right. It traveled no more than six inches before it detonated on the tip of Moorer's chin.

Moorer crumpled onto his back and remained there, staring at but not seeing the ceiling, and referee Joe Cortez counted over him. When Cortez tolled 10, George Foreman went to his knees in prayer.

The ring was engulfed by berserk fans. Strangers embraced one another.

This was a universally popular triumph. George Foreman has made himself beloved. Both 70-year-olds and 17-year-olds exult. People who never watch boxing like the fat old man.

This is for all the people in nursing homes, the new champion said. For all the people who wish upon a star. Strange, but it didn't sound hokey at all when you listened to him saying it.

They will come for him now, the sponsors with their endorsements, begging him, and soon we will be awash in paeans to the defiance of age.

He will almost surely defend his title, certainly against someone carefully handpicked. Styles make fights, and Michael Moorer was tailor-made for George Foreman because he stands in front of you and offers neither movement nor angle. And as a left–hander, he is susceptible to the short right lead, which is the old man's best punch.

It doesn't matter when he fights next. Or whom. He will milk this, and he is entitled to. Because he has made sports fun again. He has made us smile again.

A nice man won for a change, and he didn't stand over his fallen foe and mock and taunt. Instead, he went to his knees to pray.

And for however brief and fleeting a moment, we were allowed to believe that we really could hold back the night.

8

Olympics . . . When All That Glitters Is Not Gold

Eric Heiden:
Eric the Gold

FEBRUARY 1980

Lake Placid, New York—It's a sweep for team Heiden. And it is obvious now that distance and weather don't matter. Eric Heiden can race you around the block or around the world and the result is the same.

Eric the Gold won number five yesterday, this one the punishing 10,000 meters, speed skating's version of the marathon. This was one race where they thought they might catch him, figuring he would be worn down by now, chased into exhaustion.

So all he did was produce a world record, by 6.2 seconds. We should all be so exhausted.

So what has the greatest gold digger in Olympics history accomplished? Well, he won five gold medals, and only two entire countries, the Soviet Union and East Germany, exceeded that. Nobody even enters five events, much less wins them all.

Gold skated 18,000 meters, or roughly 11 miles. He won sprints and middle distances and marathons; he won in snow and wind and sun and cold and sleet and slush. Clearly, he is a man for all seasons… and distances. What he did was like a track star winning the quarter, the half, the mile, the two-mile and the marathon. And you're right. Nobody has ever done that.

Nobody had ever won five individual gold medals in *any* Olympics— Winter, Summer, high altitude, below sea level, anywhere, any time. And yes, Mark Spitz did collect seven golds, but three of them were on relays. Eric Heiden does strictly a single.

Perhaps the most remarkable aspect of his Olympics is that through all of the frenzy and madness, he remained so laid back, so unaffected. There seems to be a lot of Pete Rose in Eric Heiden. He feeds off the pressure and the crowds and the energy and the expectations. Some athletes are suffocated by it; Eric Heiden seems to thrive on it. It stokes him.

He was, for example, so uptight about the 10,000 that he overslept.

"I was supposed to get up at 6:30," he said somewhat sheepishly. "At 20 to eight they were pounding on the door, wanting to know where I was. So I ran by the cafeteria, grabbed three slices of bread and hurried to the track."

Whereupon he found himself paired with the world record holder in the 10,000, a strapping Russian named Viktor Ljoskin. And he looked up at the electronic scoreboard while he was wolfing down his three-slice breakfast, swallowed hard, and found that the first pair had already shattered the Olympic record.

A Norwegian, Tom Erik Oxholm, had put a sizzling 14 minutes, 36.60 seconds on the board, almost seven seconds faster than Eric Heiden had ever skated the 10,000 before yesterday. Eric swallowed hard again.

"Oxholm already has a 14:36 in the bank, and geez, I was figuring I could win with about a 14:40," Heiden said. "God, I was scared."

He went out at a 14:30 pace, which is inhuman. Ljoskin went out even faster, and led Heiden for half of the 25-lap race. But the rest of the way, as the Russian faded, Heiden actually picked up the pace, and finished in 14:28.13, and a full half a lap ahead of Ljoskin, who was in agony.

"It hurt," Eric the Gold admitted. "The last five laps all I could think about was how good it would feel when I could stand up."

A big, powerful Dutchman, Piet Kleine, the 1976 champion, came along later to take the silver in 14:36.03, while Oxholm's time held up for the bronze. Mike Woods of the U.S., who skated with Oxholm in the first pair, was fourth in 14:39.53. It was the only time during these Olympics that the man paired with Heiden hadn't ridden his jet stream and been carried to second place.

"It's good to skate with Eric," Oxholm had said. "That way, you get the silver."

So after turning the speed skating oval into his own personal Lost Dutchman Mine, just how impressed was Eric the Gold with himself and his unprecedented five gold medals? Not very.

"I guess I'll put them with the rest of the trophies and stuff. In my mom's dresser. They'll collect dust. The medals just don't mean that much to me in themselves. What can you do with them? I'd rather win a nice warm-up suit, something I can use. Maybe I'll sell them when I'm old and I need money."

There was nothing arrogant in his answers, or flippant. It's just that he seems to be able to maintain a perspective about all of this, even if nobody else can.

"Before the Olympics, I thought I might win maybe one or two golds," he said. "But five, I thought that was out of the question. And the 10,000, that was the last world record I ever expected to break."

So Eric the Gold surprised even himself.

Someone wanted to know if the President had called him. Heiden shrugged.

"I kinda disconnected my phone," he said. "Maybe there'll be a message to call him when I get home. I've never been to Washington. It's something to do, I guess."

And what is the allure of speed skating? All you do, it was suggested, is go around and around and around.

"I like to get dizzy," he said, grinning. "No, seriously, I enjoy it so much because it's just you and how hard you work. You don't have to rely on something mechanical to go fast."

"Sometimes, when I'm really stroking strong, I can feel the ice breaking away under me. It's a great feeling because it means I have reached the limit; the ice can't hold me any more."

In the Scandinavian countries, Eric the Gold is a god. The hottest selling song in Norway is "The Ballad of Eric." The Norwegians futilely chased him at Lake Placid, and yesterday gladly conceded unconditional surrender.

"I accept that he is the best," said the Norwegian speed–skating coach, Arne Lier. "There is no other choice. This last year, I trained four of my boys the way Eric trained. One of them collapsed."

"You cannot," Arne Lier said wisely, "make a race horse from a farm horse. Eric was born a race horse."

Whiteface—Stenmark:
The Mountain Man

FEBRUARY 20, 1980

Wilmington, New York—The closest thing to the Giant Slalom is sliding on a banana peel down a spiral staircase. You zig-zag four–fifths of a mile, over a glacier of man-made glaze, fighting the gravity of a vertical drop of one-third of a mile, and if that's not enough to clear your sinuses, you have to weave your way through a maze of 56 gates on the way down.

It's a little like staggering home at three in the morning with a load on, and trying to tiptoe through your darkened house without waking the little woman…only you found out she rearranged the furniture. Hit the sofa and you get a bruised shin, plus a lecture. Make a boo-boo in the Giant Slalom, however, and you can hold an autograph party for your plaster cast.

Only one man in the world makes the GS look no more difficult than, say, threading a needle. He is Ingemar Stenmark, Sweden's winterized version of Bjorn Borg.

Nobody can remember the last time Stenmark lost a GS. It's been more than two years. But there was thick suspense clogging Whiteface Mountain yesterday in the Winter Olympics, for after the first half of the Giant Slalom, Stenmark was not in the lead. He wasn't even second.

But it all turned out to be a tease.

Stenmark is so good, so effortless, such a technician and a stylist, that it almost seems he toys with the field, lets his pursuers rush to an early lead, builds false hope and then cruelly crushes it with a second-day blitz.

That was precisely what he did yesterday in winning the gold medal in the GS at Whiteface.

You remember Whiteface from the downhill last week. Good ol' ugly, nasty Whiteface, buster of dreams, breaker of bodies. But she became helpless putty in the experienced hands of Ingemar Stenmark.

He romanced that mean old hag, and she melted under his caress. The other skiers tried to overpower her; they are dive-bombers. But Stenmark has a lyrical flow; the others get down a boogie while the Swede makes his descent a glide, swooping so gracefully he seems actually to be going slower than everyone else. That, of course, is the secret of all the great ones in any sport.

But there is a controlled ferocity behind his rhythmically swirling runs.

"You must attack," he said, "on three fronts. You must attack the mountain and the gates and the clock."

That, incidentally, is something of a monologue for Stenmark, the Silent Swede who makes Garbo look like a gadabout. Mostly, Stenmark's remarks are limited to "Dat's gut." Or, "Dat's not."

Alpine skiing is strictly jet-set stuff—chalets and guys with monocles and hyphenated names. Cars and women, each with a chassis that makes you breathe fast. But Stenmark shuns all of this. He is happiest, he says running in the woods with his dog. The dog is named Zorro. Somehow that seems appropriate, for Stenmark carves up mountains, leaving his personal "Z" branched on them.

He had dominated his sport so thoroughly that he single-handedly caused a change in the scoring system. It was kind of like the old days when they kept crying, "Break up the Yankees."

It didn't seem to faze him. His nerves must be Swedish steel. They reach 50 miles an hour, and always there are the turns, the constant transfer of weight. Stenmark trains for them by riding a unicycle and by walking a tightrope strung across his backyard.

It is a sport of balance, and the hardest part is to learn not to fight the turns but to flow with them, to snuggle your track into the contour of the mountain.

With Whiteface, that is not too easy. In the first GS run on Monday, 14 of the skiers wiped out; yesterday, an Italian lost it. And then a Russian spilled at the bottom, plowing through the final gate and separating his shoulder. On this same course a year ago, America's Phil Mahre shattered his ankle so badly that the bone was exposed. He needed a metal plate and seven screws to hold it together. Phil Mahre was out there racing again yesterday.

Ingemar Stenmark knows the treachery of mountains. Last September, in Italy, he was in a downhill race and was caught up in a gust of wind. The crash knocked him unconscious, and he was hospitalized for a week. Eight million Swedes demanded he make a public pledge to never ski downhill again. They wanted him whole for the GS and for the slalom, not pressed into some Swedish meatball by the downhill grinder.

"I make this public promise," Stenmark had said, "that I will never run downhill again."

You could hear the sigh of relief from Stockholm to Göteborg.

And then, impishly, puckishly, Ingemar Stenmark added: "And I also promise that if I *do* run downhill again, I will not fall."

Whiteface—Mahre:
Revenge on Whiteface

FEBRUARY 23, 1980

Lake Placid, New York—The mountain had shattered his ankle, smashed it like kindling wood. The surgeon put it back together with a metal plate and seven screws.

Yesterday, Phil Mahre got even with the mountain.

And the U.S. men's alpine skiing team, which has seen nothing but "Shutout City" on the Olympics slope for the last 16 years, finally had itself a medal.

Phil Mahre slashed his skis across Whiteface Mountain as if he were using a switchblade, and he won the silver medal in the men's slalom of the 1980 Winter Olympics. He almost won the gold.

He had careened through the steep, 60-gate maze in the first run with the fastest time of 83 starters. But on the second run, he was overtaken by a familiar figure. Ingemar Stenmark, the Swedish Shadow, swooped from back in the pack, as he always does, and took the gold, with a combined time for two runs of one minute, 44.26 seconds.

But Mahre held together for second place, exactly one-half of a second behind the silky Swede, and three-tenths of a second ahead of Jacques Luethy of Switzerland, the bronze medalist. Austria, for a change, was blanked.

It was the second gold for Stenmark at these games, following his Giant Slalom triumph. He might have pulled off a Jean-Claude Killy-style triple but for the fact that following a concussion in training for the downhill last fall, he decided to pass up that event, in which he has rarely done well.

And Mahre's silver was the first men's alpine skiing medal for the U.S. since Billy Kidd was schussing out from under his cowboy hats in the 1964 Olympics.

It was sweet for Mahre, coming on the same slopes where, last March, he had spilled, costing him a chance for the World Cup and breaking an ankle.

Mahre still carries three of those screws and that metal plate around in his ankle. They will be surgically removed in April. Until then, he is left with a decided limp when he is not on skis.

"I just made up my mind that all the rehabilitation, all the training and work I had gone through after that fall, well, there was no sense going out there timid and settling for a comfortable fifth or sixth," he said.

"I figured this was the last race, why play it cozy, and if I went o.c. [out of control], that was still better than cruising down and not getting anything and then spending the rest of my life wondering what would have happened if I'd just floored it."

He floored it the first run, earning the fastest time. That was important because it assured him of an early seeding for the second run. It snowed on Whiteface yesterday, all during the race. And that, combined with all the traffic, made the course rutty after the first few racers had gone down. It was a help to ski early. All three medalists, for example, came from the first half dozen competitors to run the course the second time.

It was a cold, bleak day, and Phil Mahre skied with a tiny, battery-controlled heater in his left boot to keep that ankle—part bone, part metal—warm.

He was cheered down the slopes by a large American crowd. The course for the men's slalom is halfway up the rugged Whiteface, but two U.S. supporters climbed it, then scaled a large tree, balanced themselves on limbs, and stretched out a banner reading: "GO FOR IT, U.S.A."

There was a lengthy delay between runs. Mahre had the better part of two hours to stand around and wait, knowing that all the time Stenmark was lurking just over his shoulder, ready to uncork his customary blazing finish. The Swede did precisely that, skiing the second run in 50.37 seconds, fastest in the field.

Mahre, who is 22 and now lives in Yakima, Washington, spent most of his waiting time by himself, gazing vacantly at the snow.

"I had no problem psyching myself up," he said. "In fact, I had just the exact opposite problem. Trying not to get too pumped. I knew Ingemar would come at me with both guns. But I sure wasn't gonna back off, not after all that happened."

Yet despite the silver medal, Mahre was quick to find flaws in his performance on the second run, in which his time of 51.85 seconds was only the eight best in the field.

"My second run was pretty frantic, "he said. "I got tangled up with a gate, and it followed me for several gates. I got really sideways later, and I almost came to a full stop. I didn't know if I was going to make it down. I never really got my rhythm."

Still, it was a pretty good day for Phil Mahre, who had to wait more than 11 months to get his revenge from Whiteface.

"Of course," he noted, "the mountain always wins. It'll still be there after I'm gone."

But for one sweet moment, the mountain had relented, and Phil Mahre had his medal.

Nadia I:
The Games Are Hers

JULY 22, 1976

Montreal—She is mostly pony tail and bangs, coltish legs and bony rib cage, hollow brown eyes and a spine like a rubber band. She seems more frail than a promise, but she moves like a sunbeam.

She is all of 14 years old, an age when the burning issues in your life are supposed to be things like when will I get rid of these braces, and won't I ever develop a bosom and what's so important about studying history, anyway?

But right now she owns the biggest sports event in the world. The Games of the 21st Olympiad belong to Nadia Comaneci.

She has confounded a computer, dazzled the judges, infuriated the opposition and left gymnastics experts muttering in consternation. She has, you see, this disconcerting habit of getting perfect scores. And, it turns out, there are some people who lapse into apoplexy when confronted with perfection. The folks at IBM had to rewire their scoring machine just to accommodate her. They put a man on the moon with less trouble.

The Russian women's gymnastics coach, Larissa Latynina, herself a former gold medalist, said archly: "Even great gymnasts have small imperfections. I am sure she and her coaches know what her imperfections are."

But Hardy Fink, technical chairman of the Canadian Gymnastics Federation, blurted: "If she doesn't win everything, then somebody is cheating."

Precisely, charge the critics. Only maybe it's not exactly cheating. It's just that the judges score her too high. Theoretically, a perfect score is not possible because that means there can be no improvement.

So the bickering rages on, clusters of badge-bedecked officials waving their arms and getting red in the face. Somewhere along the line, they seem to have lost their perspective. Ye gods, all this fuss over someone confronting puberty?

The most unexcited person in this whole controversy appears to be Nadia Comaneci herself. They argue, she calmly explodes another sunburst of aerial acrobatics, and sits down. Oh, she smiles and she waves, neither of which she used to do, but it does not seem spontaneous, rather practiced, like a maneuver on the balance beam.

She is very solemn for a 14-year-old, and I cannot help but feel sorry for her. Because 14-year-old girls are supposed to giggle and practice flirting and whisper to each other, holding up their hands to their mouths. She is the best in the world, but what terrible price has she had to pay? If one must practice smiling, if a simple grin is not something that has happened naturally, then it is not worth it, not for all the gold medals ever struck.

"It is in her nature to be serious," says Bela Karolyi, the coach of the Romanian team.

He is her Svengali. He found her in a kindergarten and he gave her his ultimate test… a walk on the beam.

"Everyone," said a gymnastics coach, "is scared on the beam. No matter how many times they've been on it, no matter how good they are, they're shaking inside."

Bela Karolyi nods in agreement. "If they are afraid of the beam, we send them home right away."

Nadia Comaneci did not go home. She stayed.

Olympic rules say only women may accompany the gymnast onto the floor during competition. So Karolyi sits in the stands and watches, and after each routine, Comaneci sneaks glances at him, seeking approval, confirmation, reassurance. Those perfect tens light up the scoreboard, and they smile and nod at each other.

"You cannot be scared," says Karolyi. "Holding back is when you get in trouble."

So Nadia Comaneci hurls herself into each flawless maneuver with marvelous abandon. And the people in the stands go absolutely berserk.

And the writers from all over the world seek an audience with her as though they were in the presence of the Queen of England, who is also here, instead of a 14-year-old girl.

And Nadia Comaneci stands very still and looks at all these crazy people through widening brown eyes and she smiles shyly, as though to say, "Why all the fuss?"

"Famous?" she repeats the question haltingly. "It's all right, I don't want to get too excited about it."

Sometimes it helps to be only 14 years old.

Nadia II:
It Does Not Compute

Montreal—On a scale of one to 10, Nadia Comaneci is an 11. The nerveless, 14-year-old Romanian with the silly–putty body completed her total captivation of the 21st Olympics last night with two more gold medals and still another perfect score in the finals of women's gymnastics.

On the uneven parallel bars, she walked to within a razor's edge of disaster with the nonchalance of a little girl playing hopscotch, and achieved her fourth straight 10.0 score.

On the scoreboard, however, it registers as 1.00. Before Comaneci, the highest possible mark had been 9.99. The computer makers will be happy to see her return to Bucharest. She forced them to rewire all their scoring circuits.

Never before had an Olympic gymnast been awarded a flawless mark. Comaneci rang up six, and she seemed the only one who wasn't excited about it.

"It is not that big a thing," she said, shrugging. "I have done it 21 times now."

Last night, she won the gold medal on the parallel bars and the balance beam, was third in floor exercise and narrowly missed another medal in the horse vault. The previous night, she had won the women's all–around gold medal.

So, hanging around the neck of a real-life Barbie doll with incredible bounce are five medals: three golds, a silver and a bronze.

If there was a crown designating the queen of the Olympics, she would wear that, too. In less than a week, she has become a global heroine, in the same manner that Olga Korbut enchanted the world at the 1972 games in Munich.

Just as Korbut overshadowed five-time world champion Ludmila Tourischeva in Munich, so did Comaneci obscure Nellie Kim of the Soviet Union. Part Asian and part Russian, Kim, 19, with balletic grace and regal dignity, won the two golds that Comaneci did not take last night, in the floor exercise and horse vault.

It was Comaneci who brought the crowd into the Forum, however, and as she performed, flashbulbs crackled like a siege of starving locusts.

Gymnastics used to be a more reserved sport, and art form really, but Korbut changed it from a night at the symphony to a night at the fireworks with her aerial daring and spritely, little-girl charm.

Comaneci has expanded on that, mixing boogaloo with ballet, some flapper and some flips, dash and danger. Her coaches, with a Madison Avenue eye for packaging, changed her musical accompaniment, making it bouncier, and they urged her to wave and smile at the crowd.

What it has earned has caused a furor among those who believe that perfection is not attainable. They have argued that no one should receive a 10.0, and they contended that the judges started marking too high from the beginning.

"She is not perfect," said one gymnastics expert, "but she is so much better than anyone else, and when the rest are being graded at 9.8 and 9.9, where else can you go? You have to go to a 10."

For her part, Comaneci has been coyly cool, oblivious to the debate with casualness well beyond her years.

Haven't you ever, she was asked, been nervous?

"Only when I fight with my brother," she giggled.

9

Golf . . .
Spelled Backward
It's F-L-O-G

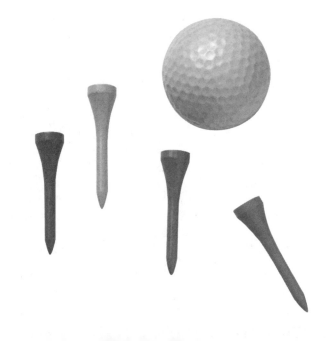

Amen Corner

APRIL 7, 2005

When they exchanged their vows all those years ago, she had told him: "I'll never worry about you taking a mistress. You already have one."

She was right.

Her name is Augusta.

Under the great spreading oak in back of the clubhouse, a most congenial spot, a Pilgrim, newly arrived in Eden, asks for directions to Amen Corner.

"I can find no signs," he laments.

And for good reason. There are none. No signs. No Interstate billboards. No exit ramps. No garish neon. This is, after all, Augusta, sedate and prim, and the Masters, unbending and implacable, and things are done in a certain, proper, prescribed, unalterable, unshakable manner, Laddy Boy, so mind your P's and Q's, wipe your feet, and use the trash receptacles, please.

Amen Corner, celebrated for all these years in lore and legend and song, is tucked away in the far corner of the soft, green folds of Augusta National, a decent hike from the clubhouse and a drop of some 14 stories, which you don't notice while strolling there but sure do experience coming back, when you begin to wheeze and huff. Or huff and wheeze.

It is surely the most famous intersection in sports. From time to time, I have suggested that if a person were so inclined, and were it legal, a person's ashes could not be scattered over a more intoxicating spot. That conviction holds.

Numbers 11, 12 and 13 come together at Amen Corner, and from the strategically positioned grandstand, it is possible to watch play, partial and complete, on all three.

Masters tournaments have been won here, and lost here, for they constitute, after all, the centerpiece of the back nine of Augusta National, and there is no greater theater than the back nine on Masters Sunday.

Amen Corner calls for prudent judgment and cautious decisions. The bold and the rash inevitably meet cruel fates, those demises almost always being of their own making. If you negotiate Amen Corner in level par, it is said, then offer up a silent prayer of gratitude, and run, don't walk, to the 14th tee. (It was the golf writer Herbert Warren Wind who christened Amen Corner, borrowing it from an old spiritual, "Shoutin' at the Amen Corner.")

Number 11 is a par four with water on the left, and the three most important commandments to remember as you stand over your second shot are: Thou shalt not be left, thou shalt not be left, thou shalt not be left.

Nick Faldo would like to bronze the 11th and take it home with him. He has won the Masters on the 11th not once but twice, both occasions being the second holes of playoffs. One of those Faldo didn't win so much as Ray Floyd lost it, for Floyd, in violation of the commandment, sent his second shot to a watery grave.

It was on the 11th—actually, well off the 11th—that Larry Mize chipped in during a playoff with the tormented Greg Norman, who was kneeling there, minding his own business and lining up the putt he intended to win the Masters with, when Mize's ball went skittering into the hole like a frightened rabbit.

The 12th is a par three, and it is nasty, nasty, nasty—a cruel little seductress that entices with promises and then cuts your heart out. The devil's own. Water in front, bunkers sprinkled about in Satanic array, and the wind . . . always the wind . . . billowing this way and that—capricious, deceptive, deceitful, reaching out to snatch a ball and deposit it in some dark, unplayable place.

The 13th is a par five, a dogleg left, and what you see from the Amen Corner grandstand is the tee ball. Make the ball hug the dogleg and the green is easily reachable in two. If the tee ball is right, it is still possible to go for the green. If you have the nerve for it.

The risk is a wet golf ball. The reward is a chance at an eagle.

Glory.

Or gloom.

Augusta never fails to deliver great drama. This year's Masters burgeons with promise, for golf appears to be enjoying a Golden Age at the moment, marked by the rise of The Big Five. No, not Penn, Villanova, Temple, La Salle and St. Joe's. Rather, Phil Mickelson, Tiger Woods, Vijay Singh, Ernie Els and Retief Goosen. Five of the finest players ever. And all gathered here, all knowing that to slip on the green jacket, they will have to traverse Amen Corner. Four times. At least.

Arnold Palmer:
The Long Goodbye

APRIL 10, 2004

At 46 minutes past noon, on a soft, sun-dappled spring afternoon in Georgia, on a golf course of unsurpassing splendor, before an enormous and worshipful gallery, the Long Goodbye began.

Arnold Palmer played his final round at Augusta National, in the tournament he made famous. And vice versa.

Five hours, 17 minutes later, he nudged in a bogey putt on his 84th and last stroke of the day, thus finishing an astonishing run in which he played in 50 Masters, which is an unfathomable and almost certainly unreachable number.

What he shot had no relevance. What was so extraordinary is that thousands upon thousands of people turned out to watch a man of 74 years play one last round and do it walking all the way, walking over a leg-punishing course of rolling, pine-tree-lined fairways and curling, azalea-scented swales.

From the veranda of the clubhouse, when you looked out toward the first tee, it looked like a Cecil B. DeMille epic, the supporting cast of thousands stretching to the horizon. And then the masses parted and Arnold Palmer walked through.

Make way for the King.

The applause was thunderous and almost without end. It carried him around his round, and he doffed his white visor and waved again and again and again, and many of them he knew, for hardly ever has an athlete had such a fiercely loyal following or reciprocated that loyalty in such loving fashion. Arnie's Army and its commander had grown old together and had done so with uncommon grace.

He is as beloved at Augusta as any other athlete in any other venue has ever been, and as he played his farewell, he bit at his lip, and when he was done, he succumbed, the tears crawling down his face.

"I'm just a sentimental slob," he said.

Tens of thousands of sentimental slobs walked with him yesterday. Many of us chose to blame the pollen for our sniffles.

Surely, no other athlete in any other sport—ever—has been able to compete in his chosen craft at such an age. And he never lost his zest for the hunt, his passion for the game. He never burned out and, indeed, talked wistfully of coming to his 50th Masters to try to make the cut, and if he managed that, why not try to win the darn thing again?

"I'm a dreamer," he said. "I continue to get up in the morning enthusiastically and pick up a golf club with a thought that I can somewhere find that secret to making another cut. That's just an example, but it applies to other things in life, too."

He has always been bull-strong, and the remarkable part of his achievement is that all 50 of his Masters were in succession. Imagine. Half a century and he never missed competing. Not once.

You know that somewhere in there was a bellyache or a cold or a bad back, something to make him stay home, to make him pull the covers over his head and say, "Not this time." But even prostate cancer could not keep him away.

No other person, venue and event are as tethered to one another as Arnold Palmer, Augusta National and the Masters.

That is why he had such a hard time letting go. He said his valedictory two years ago, without really planning or meaning it, then changed his mind when the Green Coats who run the tournament agreed to reinstate lifetime playing exemptions. They told him they'd be honored to have him around for a couple more Masters.

And why not? He is guaranteed box office, guaranteed TV ratings.

If the Masters has been with us forever, Arnold Palmer has been with us almost forever, first as the rakish, risk-taking, swashbuckling hard charger who had the good sense of timing to come along at the same time as television.

The money soon followed. Buckets of it. Even today, players acknowledge that he is the one who lit the golden lamp for them, and to him they owe a debt of gratitude beyond paying.

"It's done," he said yesterday when he met with the media. "It's not fun, but it's time for it to be done. I'm cooked."

But he is done at Augusta only as a player. He will still return for the champions dinner and to kibitz and, perhaps, to serve as honorary starter.

"It would be empty for me not to be here," he said. "I don't think I could ever separate myself from this tournament, from this place."

His caddie for the Long Goodbye was his grandson. Samuel Palmer Saunders is 16 and a golfer so good that he won the club championship at Bay Hill last year. Grandpa bought the course some years ago.

Earlier this week, Arnold Palmer was asked what had been his very best day on a golf course, and he smiled that engaging, crooked grin and said: "A single day? I've had 50 years of single days."

A lucky man. And, more, one who knows he is.

Jack Nicklaus:
The Masters' Master

APRIL 10, 2005

On a soft, spring day in Georgia, on one of those impossibly green fairways on the course that makes you feel as if you're standing at heaven's gate, as he prepared for his second shot from a cruel hanging lie on that punishingly steep, uphill number nine, the greatest golfer who ever lived began to cry.

"He asked me for a towel," his caddie said.

"He couldn't talk," the oldest son of Jack Nicklaus said.

"I told him," Jackie Nicklaus added, "that I loved him."

And then they began the walk up to the green of the last hole that Jack Nicklaus will play in the Masters, the tournament that he played in for 45 years and dominated for more than half that time.

Jack Nicklaus had made his decision—or, rather, had had it made for him by his struggles with the game that used to come so easily for him—but he had not formally announced that yesterday's was to be his final competitive round at Augusta National. The spectators seemed to sense it, though, for they rose as one and accorded him a sustained, tear-streaked ovation.

Jack Nicklaus has always done things on his own terms, and now he was going out the way he wanted, making the most difficult decision a great athlete has to make—determining when enough is enough.

In a typically blunt, unsparing self-assessment, he said: "I'm an old man trying to figure out some way to get out of the way." That is the way life works, the natural order of things, an immutable progression.

"It's all right," he said. "I accept that. We should move aside, make way."

You had the feeling this was coming as you watched him play the last two rounds. The man who once pulverized the ball, the man who brought courses to their knees, had seen his powers wane and melt away. It happens.

He is 65, tilts to one side because of a hip replacement, and is plagued by a back that makes walking the hills and swales of Augusta National torture. And to bend to take the ball out of the cup, he first must take a deep breath.

He shot 77-76, and he was no threat to make the cut.

"That's about five under par for me," the man who had played 71 rounds under par at Augusta said. "Probably as good as I'm going to play on this golf course, with the conditions and the length.

"It's great and it's fun to play in the Masters, but it's certainly no fun to play this way. It's no fun to go out there and hack it around and struggle to try to figure out some way to break 80. That's never been the way I've operated, and I don't believe I should be out there."

It was Bobby Jones, another golfing titan, who once offered what has become the definitive summation of Jack Nicklaus: "He plays a game with which I'm unfamiliar."

And the poignant irony is that now Jack Nicklaus finds himself, to his great, gnashing frustration, playing a game with which he is unfamiliar. So he wrestles with his ego and his competitive furies and he arrives at a judgment. The greater you are, the harder that is.

He said he had no particular interest in a farewell tour, in giving his public a chance to say goodbye. But despite his failing game and assorted infirmities, he did say he would likely participate in a Masters old-timers game if one was organized and played from tees that would not humiliate past champions. It's such a good idea, you wonder why nobody ever thought of it before.

Nicklaus' two favorite courses are Augusta National and St. Andrews. Serendipitously, the British Open is being played at St. Andrews this year, and that, he said, will be his final tournament.

Though he seemed to close the door, he didn't lock it entirely, saying that he could always change his mind. But for that to happen, he would need to find 10 miles per hour more on his swing and the Masters directors would have to shorten the holes by 30 yards.

"Ain't gonna happen," he said.

The end came on number nine rather than number 18 because rain delays have made this the "Never-Ending Masters," players being sent off the number one and number 10 tees to catch up, to make the traditional Sunday finish possible.

Jack Nicklaus hit that shot from the hanging lie at number nine with a six-iron, the ball stopping only four feet below the hole. The gallery, of course, went bonkers. He wanted to go out with a birdie, but he kept wiping his eyes. His playing partner, Jay Haas, was fighting tears, too.

He missed the putt.

The tap-in for par was stroke number 11,733 in his 163 rounds at Augusta, where he won six times and finished second four times and third twice. No other player ever had such a stranglehold on a tournament.

He first arrived at Augusta when he was 19, the son of an Ohio pharmacist, single and cocky. Now he is a father five times over, with 16 grandchildren, and weeks removed from the unspeakable tragedy of losing a grandchild in a drowning accident.

This tournament was suggested by his second-oldest son, Steve, the father of 17-month-old Jake, as a way of softening the hurt, a closure of sorts.

Steve will caddie for his father at St. Andrews. He and Jackie decided on the rotation between them—Jackie on the bag at Augusta, Steve at the cradle of golf.

"I asked them if I had a say, and they said no," Jack Nicklaus recalled.

He didn't argue. That, too, is part of the progression, the way of things.

Tiger Woods:
Walking with Giants

APRIL 11, 2005

For four hours and 32 minutes, through the shadow-streaked splendor of Augusta National, they had waged a magnificent duel in the sun, just the two of them, the rest of the field having been left in hopeless arrears, and now it was the first hole of sudden death and Tiger Woods was trying to stare down a nasty, 15-foot slider for a birdie.

And for the Masters.

With a bold and decisive pass of his putter, he curled it in, and finally had shaken himself loose from the dogged, determined grip of Chris Di-Marco, a most worthy opponent and a man who revealed himself to be made of true grit.

And thus did Eldrick T. Woods win his fourth green jacket, all of them within the last nine years, and in the process reestablish himself as the best golfer in the world. With, presumably, the best still to come. For he is not yet 30 and has won four Masters, a number equaled only by Arnold Palmer and exceeded only by Jack Nicklaus' six. So he walks with the giants.

After a "slump" in which he failed to win a major championship in the last $2^1/_2$ years, Woods has banked his ninth biggie. It moves him halfway to Nicklaus' record of 18 majors, which was once thought uncatchable.

But then Woods himself has been virtually uncatchable when he has had the lead in his teeth. Before yesterday, his record when leading tournaments going into the final round was 30-3. In the majors, an even more daunting 8-0. Intimidating stuff, indeed.

And when he made a freight-train rush past a dazed DiMarco in the third round yesterday, sinking seven birdies in a row, zooming from four shots out of the lead to three shots ahead, the popular assumption was that this Masters Sunday would be another Tiger walkover. Having shot 66-65 in the middle two rounds, surely he had cowed the rest of the field.

And when he stepped to the first tee to launch the final round, he wore what Vietnam vets call the thousand-yard stare, looking at something only he could see, something off on the horizon or beyond, and he unsheathed his thermonuclear driver and whaled a tee ball that traveled three and a half football fields—$349^1/_2$ yards to be exact. Which is ridiculous. Di-Marco's ball was 61 yards behind.

But DiMarco swallowed hard and proved to be all bulldog. He would not be subdued, he would not melt away like so many of Tiger Woods' victims. And it was Woods who was doing the stumbling in the stretch, bogeying the last two holes when only one par would have presented him with the win.

Woods ended up shooting a final-round 71. DiMarco shot a gutsy 68. Their closest pursuers were seven strokes behind.

They played number 18 in sudden death. DiMarco's second shot on the par-four hole finished short of the green, but he made a lovely chip to tap-in distance. Woods' approach shot landed 15 feet above the cup.

It was in almost the exact same position as Phil Mickelson's ball on the 72nd hole of last year's Masters. Mickelson rolled his putt in. So did Woods. For birdie. Woods, too. For the green coat. Woods, too.

Woods and DiMarco, and the rest of the field, had to finish their third rounds early yesterday morning, wait a bit and then go back out. The schedule was scrambled all four days because of incessant rain delays. It was constant, unsettling catch-up, and difficult to find a rhythm.

Woods birdied the last three holes of the front nine on Saturday but then had to go sleep on it, play being halted due to darkness. Probably he had lost momentum by then, right? Ha! He proceeded to birdie the first four holes on the back nine. It was quite a display of concentration and perseverance.

But DiMarco was just as adept at collecting himself. After collapsing with a back-nine 41, he shot that 68, and did it when paired with Woods.

"He is one heck of a tough competitor," Woods said. "He played beautifully all day. There's no back-off in him."

DiMarco simply would not let go. Which, Woods said, was fine with him.

"It was a fun day, all in all," he added.

And so it was, a wild, turbulent day of glorious improvisation and of bone-headed, ham-handed misjudgments. In other words, it was what Masters Sunday always is—great, riveting drama in an amphitheater of unsurpassed beauty. No other sporting event delivers such remarkable theater year after year.

Woods contributed a shot for the ages, one that will endure in the memory bank, a chip-in birdie two on the 16th. He played pasture pool from the fringe of the second cut, feathering the ball off the crest of the green and watching it trickle down, down, down, pausing on the lip of the cup.

And then, after a hiccup or two, the ball decided to fall in. You assumed that was the tournament, for it gave him a two-shot lead with two holes to play. But he finished bogey-bogey and backed up.

But only until sudden death. He has won 43 PGA tournaments. That is seventh all-time. This one, he set apart.

"This is for Dad," he said, his voice breaking.

Earl Woods, who had his son playing golf when he was three years old, is gravely ill.

"I really wanted to win this one for him," Woods said. "Maybe give him a little more fire to keep fighting."

And the newest Masters champion used a sleeve of the green coat to swipe away the tears.

Ball from 9/11:
A Dimpled Survivor

JUNE 13, 2002

He was running a rake through the debris of ground zero when his eye was caught by a flash of white.

Bone, he thought. Lord knows, he'd seen enough of those. But no. Not bone. Ball. A golf ball, shining like a pearl in that awful, dark desolation.

John Caputo, a New York City fireman, bent, picked it up, and then the golfer in him took over. On instinct, he licked a thumb and began to clean it.

"And then," he said, "I thought, 'Whoa, what are you doing?'"

It felt like something close to blasphemy.

Yesterday, Caputo presented that golf ball, survivor of 9-11, retrieved from the wreckage of the South Tower of the World Trade Center, to the United States Golf Association for display in its museum.

It's a Titleist. With a red number four. How it did not get crushed is beyond all plausible explanation. A building, a giant colossus of a building, fell on it, and yet it survived. Unbendable steel bent, unbreakable beams broke, and things were vaporized on that terrible, terrible morning, yet a new golf ball, somehow, stayed whole.

It is neither lopsided nor dented nor cut. The dimples are splotched with the brown sprinklings of dust, but otherwise it could have just come out of a fresh sleeve.

The symbolism inherent in this causes people to crowd around it and stare with a hushed reverence, as though it were a religious object.

You look at it and it makes something well within you, a geyser of pride.

For like the city in which it was entombed, like this country, it is still here, and defiantly, thunderingly so. Or, as New York Governor George Pataki said at yesterday's presentation: "We're back, and better than ever."

The USGA is holding its Open championship, which begins today on a public course. It is the first time in the tournament's 102 years that the people's Open is being held on a people's course. And Bethpage, which is located in the middle of Long Island, is about 50 miles from ground zero.

The golf ball that survived 9-11 seemed most appropriate.

"It was April 1st when I found it," Caputo said. "I looked at it and I just smiled. Isn't that something?"

Isn't it?

Like a lot of firefighters and police, Caputo plays golf. He's been among the participants of Midnight Madness, which is what they call the fanatics who sleep in their cars so they can be first off the tee at any of the five courses at Bethpage.

"I had a 10 handicap once upon a time," he said. "Now it's unrecognizable."

There was a pause and then, like a true golfer, he told of his greatest moment: "I did have a hole–in–one here. On the Fourth of July."

Another pause, and then, just to keep the record straight: "It was on the Yellow course, though, not the Black one."

There are four red letters on the golf ball that John Caputo found when he was raking through the debris: NYSA. New York Shipping Association.

Headquarters: 20th floor, South Tower, World Trade Center. Correction: former headquarters.

"But everyone got out," said Beverly Fedorko of the NYSA.

"We had 42 dozen of those golf balls made up, for charities, tournaments, events like that. We'd already given about 12 dozen away. They were kept in a closet in the president's office."

She smiled.

"What do you suppose the odds were on that one surviving?"

The white-haired man who stood for pictures during the presentation ceremony yesterday was John Vigiano, a captain in the FDNY, and something of a legend. He lost two sons—Joseph, a policeman, and John, a fireman—on 9-11.

On the breast of his dress blues, Caputo wore a badge that had a picture of the Vigiano boys.

Caputo lives in Hauppauge, a village not far from Bethpage. On the morning of 9-11, he saw the South Tower on TV in flames, saw the second suicide plane slice into the North Tower. He was 50 miles away, but it didn't matter.

"Deb, I've got to go down there," he told his wife. "I've just got to."

Debbie Caputo ran to the front door and blocked him. She would not be budged.

"I'm sure she saved my life," Caputo said yesterday, his voice choking.

And then, almost seven months later, raking through the remnants of hell, that flash of white caught his eye and he fished out of the wreckage, of all things, a golf ball.

This silly little thing that we hit at and chase after and curse.

You look at it now and you swear that it glows like a candle.

10

Basketball . . . Playing Above the Rim

PhillyBall

FEBRUARY 6, 2002

Wilt, of course. And Doc. We start with them as our cornerstones of PhillyBall.

It's been almost 30 years since he played, yet even now, Wilton Norman Chamberlain owns page after page in the NBA record books. It's been more than two years since his death, yet he is still considered the most dominant player ever. He could do pretty much whatever he pleased, and the rest of them were helpless against him. If there had been even a little of the bully in him, the result would have been frightening. Nobody, he once said, loves Goliath. He spent a career trying to change that.

Julius Winfield Erving 2nd took his last flight in 1987. His legacy is that he saved one league (the NBA) and kept another (the ABA) afloat. He popularized the single most entertaining shot in the sport. He made a fast game even faster. He defined free-form basketball, gave it a soaring, sweeping elegance, and spawned a whole generation of cloud-hopping, air-walking imitators. He was also the game's spokesman, ambassador and diplomat. Other than that, he didn't have much of an impact on the sport at all.

The Big Dipper and Dr. J. They are the opening stanzas in our ode to basketball in Philadelphia. One was raw, shattering power. The other was velvet grace.

If you are a hoop head, then this is the city for you. Philadelphia dotes on football; it strains mightily to stay loyal to baseball, and it lavishes cult adoration on hockey. But basketball. . . . Ah, here we have an embarrassment of riches. A long, proud heritage. A roll call studded with marquee names. Storied arenas. A fertile breeding ground of future stars.

Like most things Philadelphian, we like our basketball on the gritty side. We like scabby knees and long, angry, red splotches caused by floor burns. Noses permanently bent by bayonet elbows. Lumps and knots, fat lips and fingers disjointed.

It is only fitting that the reigning king of basketball in this city is a little pine knot whose fearlessness is without boundary. To repeat an earlier contention here, and one that has gone unchallenged: Allen Iverson is, pound for pound and inch for inch, the toughest athlete you have ever seen.

There is rarely a part of him that isn't strained, sprained, fractured, swollen or leaking blood. He plays anyway. And never, ever backs down.

Pure PhillyBall.

It is a tradition and a legacy that goes back—way back—to a time when it was regarded as some sort of sacred responsibility to lavish nicknames on players. Hence: Jumpin' Joe Fulks, Pitchin' Paul Arizin and The Kangaroo Kid, a.k.a. Billy C.

William John Cunningham is listed in the *NBA Register* twice. Under "All-time great players" and "All-time great coaches."

He came from Brooklyn, where he had learned the asphalt game, and that style was perfectly suited for Philadelphia. He was a left–handed gun, a springy leaper, a sudden infusion of electricity off the bench as the sixth man.

After Cunningham shredded a knee, he turned to coaching. In eight seasons under him, the 76ers rolled up 454 wins against only 196 defeats, and in 1983, they won their last NBA championship.

He coached exactly the way he played, jumping from his seat with such vigor and force that, on one occasion, he split the seat of his trousers.

Even now, you close your eyes and the Wayback Machine takes you to Billy C stomping his foot while calling out: "A-n-d-r-e-w-w-w-w-w-w-w!"

And Andrew Toney, alias the Boston Strangler, would look up innocently, his expression asking: "Something I did wrong?"

Toney was bloodless and nerveless. He killed the Celtics, especially in Boston, at a time when the Sixers–Celtics was the best rivalry in the NBA and, indeed, in all of sport.

The Sixers would isolate Toney on the wing, and some unfortunate soul would crouch in front of him, utterly at his mercy. Toney's first step was a precursor of Iverson's. It made a cobra look slow.

The greatest team ever in the NBA played in this city. The 1966-67 Sixers went 68-13. They would have mashed Michael Jordan's best Bulls team and the best of the Lakers and the Celtics, too.

Wilt was the center. The man who scored 100 in one game. And who scored 78 and 73 and 72 in other games. Who averaged 50 in a season. Who averaged 23 rebounds in his career. Who never fouled out of a game. Who, in response to criticism that "all" he could do was score and rebound, announced before one season began that he would lead the league in assists—and did.

The forwards were muscular Luke Jackson and Chet "The Jet" Walker. Wali Jones, with that herky-jerky, recoil-and-reload jumper from another area code, was one guard. Hal Greer was the other. He still holds the franchise record for points in a career. And he jump-shot his free throws and made eight of every 10.

Billy C averaged 18.5 points a game that season.

The successors to that team didn't fare nearly so well. And in the 1972-73 season, the Sixers established a still-standing record for defeats that other teams have, from time to time, made inglorious runs at.

That Sixers team went 9-73.

The captain and leading scorer was Fred Carter, who raged against defeat and who resisted it steadfastly but, alas, to no avail. All you need to know about his ferocity, about why he fit in Philly, is his nickname: Mad Dog.

As penance for '72-'73, he was made to serve as coach just as the franchise was slip-sliding downhill.

Before that demise, though, there was a golden age. It stretched from the mid-1970s well into the '80s.

George McGinnis, with a physique you could strike a match on, was imported and played dutifully until the boo-birds found him unworthy.

Doc came on board, and as Pat Williams, then the Sixers' general manager, explained it: "The New Jersey Nets couldn't afford him any longer. So I went to our owner, Fitz Dixon, and said: 'We have a chance to get Julius Erving!' And Fitz, who wasn't really up on basketball, said: 'Fine and dandy, Pat. Now tell me, who is Julius Erving?'

"And I said: 'Well, he's kind of the Babe Ruth of basketball.'"

He cost six million dollars. It was a steal.

Erving's first Sixers team turned into quite a collection. It included Darryl Dawkins, a teenage Godzilla who shattered backboards. And Doug Collins, the one who coaches Air Jordan now and whose first exposure to basketball in Philly was an elbow that sliced open his face. As the blood flowed, he was told: "Make the free throws first, Doug, and then we'll sew you up."

Welcome to PhillyBall.

There was the moon-shot jump shot of Lloyd Free, who honed his stroke by the light of the moon in the Brownsville section of Brooklyn, original home of mean streets. He legally changed his name to World B. Free.

Later, there was Bobby Jones, the White Shadow, who could change a game without scoring a single point.

Then came a mouthy, hilarious, wide load from Auburn—Charles Wade Barkley. He could get a rebound while loosening the teeth of three defenders and then run a solo fastbreak the other way, dribbling behind his back and finishing it off with a thunder dunk. No one wanted to step in front of him and take a charging foul.

The city loved Barkley. He was quintessential PhillyBall. Once, he dunked so fiercely that he moved everything—basket, backboard, the whole support. The game had to be delayed while everything was put back in alignment.

The tragic irony was that, though he played for two other teams, his career ended in the city where it began, with a horrendous knee injury. He still makes a home here.

And Moses. Can't forget Moses. He did indeed lead the Sixers to the Promised Land. For all that talent they had, it took the acquisition of Moses Eugene Malone to produce a title.

He was relentless and indefatigable on the boards, the best offensive rebounder I've ever seen. Before the '83 playoffs, he uttered a public prophecy that became part of the lore of PhillyBall: "fo' . . . fo' . . . fo'. "

He was close. The Sixers won 12 in those playoffs and lost one fo' . . . five . . . fo'.

The stuff of legend.

There's more. Lots more. Like all of the places to play roundball in Philadelphia. Including the walk-up gyms where the baseline is the wall and you learn to dunk and brace at the same time.

Of all the arenas, though, one will steal your heart away.

The Palestra. The perfect little snake pit.

The crowd is on top of you. The roof is crosshatched with soaring steel trusses that look like a whale's ribs. It is hot. Noisy. Steamy.

A passionate game should be played in a passion pit. So it is encouraging to see the Big Five return to its roots, staging a tripleheader in that sweet, smelly old amphitheater.

And that's another unique part of PhillyBall. Five major college teams whose campuses are within 20 miles of one another. Drexel always gets mentioned apart, but it sits cheek by jowl with the Palestra.

And then there are those who don't play the game but are an integral part of the fabric of PhillyBall.

Sonny Hill, the godfather of basketball in this town: dresses like a boulevardier, conducts summer leagues and summer camps, and exerts more influence on players than any other person in Philadelphia.

Herb Magee: The Shootist. He played for and he still coaches what used to be Philadelphia Textile and now is Philadelphia University. He piles up the wins like snowflakes, and he can still beat you at H-O-R-S-E, spotting you the H and the O and the R and the S. If you want to learn how to put a round, pebble-grained ball through an orange rim and cotton netting, Magee's your man.

Speedy Morris: He coached high school first. Then college women. Then college men. Now he's back with the preps. He is PhillyBall. And he and his son have a vaudeville-style act, for beef-and-beers, that has funded an awful lot of charities and other worthy causes, a reminder that Philly-Ball is not limited to dribbling and dunking alone.

There are others, of course. Dozens. Scores. Hundreds.

Every enchanted once in a while, time and circumstance will converge at the same intersection, and when that happens, there is a once-in-a-generation occurrence. Such a mystical moment was created by the Sixers last spring. They galvanized the city and crossed generations and agendas and cultures.

What endeared the team to the city was PhillyBall. The passion and abandon of their play. Their extraordinary threshold of pain. Their absolute refusal to surrender.

Each game, it seemed, one of them would break a bone and play on anyway.

Iverson explained it thus: "We just throw our hearts out there on the floor."

Yes, and sometimes forget to pick them up.

They scrapped all the way to the NBA Finals. And while they didn't win the championship, they won over the city, a tough town with a low tolerance for losing.

But PhillyBall plays here because the city will put its arms around anyone, any team, that tries.

It's not the getting knocked down that captures and captivates us. It's the getting back up.

There used to be a sign in the Palestra that summed up PhillyBall: "To win the game is great. To play the game is even greater. But to love the game is greatest of all."

Amen.

Cheeks and the Anthem: Mo to the Rescue

APRIL 29, 2003

There she stood at center court, this little girl with the big, big voice, poised for the moment of a lifetime, the house lights dimmed, 20,000 people waiting expectantly for her, 20,000 people ready to hear her sing . . . and the words wouldn't come.

They lodged in her throat and couldn't be budged, no matter how mightily she strained. It was the song she knew by heart, the one she had heard a million times, the one she had sung over and over and over, the very one that she had rehearsed in a dressing room perfectly—every single run-through dead solid perfect—only minutes before for heaven's sake. But now the words all tumbled over each other, crazy-quilted, in a jumbling, confusing mish-mash: rocket's last gleaming . . . twilight's red glare . . . flag's not there . . . oh say can you see . . . yet wave . . . .

She wanted to disappear, of course. She wanted the floor to open up and swallow her. Or a spaceship to beam her up and carry her off. Natalie Gilbert, a 13-year-old eighth grader, was living the nightmare each of us, in moments of morbid, fearful imagining, has conjured.

And then suddenly, silent as a shadow, he was there, standing beside her, his left arm protectively, comfortingly around her, and he was whispering the forgotten words, and she began to nod her head—yes, yes, I remember now—and she began to mouth the words, and then he started to sing them, softly, and she joined in, hesitantly at first, but with a growing confidence, and soon they were a duet, and he was urging the crowd on with his right hand, and soon the duet had 20,000 back-ups, 20,000 people singing partly out of relief, partly out of compassion, partly out of pride, and rarely has the National Anthem of the United States of America been rendered with such heartfelt gusto.

It was a glorious, redemptive moment. Surely, you thought, sport has never been grander.

In fact, it says here that, for all the acrobatic, aeronautic, pyrotechnic, cruise-o-matic moments that the NBA playoffs have presented to us thus far this spring, all pale in comparison to the night of April 25th, in the Rose Garden in Portland, Oregon, shortly before the Trail Blazers met the Dallas Mavericks in the third game of their series.

That is when Maurice Cheeks, once the quintessential point guard, selfless and without ego and pretense, for many meritorious seasons a 76er, and most recently the coach of the Blazers, came to the rescue of Natalie Gilbert.

"I don't know why I did it," he said. "It wasn't something I thought about. It's one of those things you just do."

Except, of course, no one else thought to do it.

Everybody else did precisely what most of us would do in such a situation—study the ceiling, develop a sudden interest in our shoes, shift from side to side, paralyzed, frozen to the spot, embarrassed for the little girl, empathizing furiously, wishing desperately that it would all end: Please, let her remember the words. Please. Somebody do something.

Maurice Cheeks, himself a father, did what all fathers, and grandfathers, too, in moments of heroic reverie, dream they would do. He tried to make the world go away.

Seeing as how his team was one loss away from elimination, he might have been expected to have other things on his mind than a junior high school girl who had won a contest to sing "The Star-Spangled Banner" before tip-off of the most crucial game of the year.

And yet there he was, not sure how exactly, walking to center court. And once there, this thought stabbed him: "I wasn't sure whether I knew the words myself," he said, laughing. "I just didn't want her to be out there all alone."

For those of us who chronicled Maurice Cheeks during his tenure in Philadelphia, what he did was totally in character. The man was never the self-absorbed prima donna so many have become. He played a spare, bare-bones, beautifully economical game, and wanted very much to disappear as soon as the game was over. He had no more a desire for the spotlight than he did for flamboyance on the court.

The best point guards are sharers and protectors and soothers. The best of them understand how to get the ball to the right people in the right place at the right time. The best of them watch out for everybody else.

Maurice Cheeks is still a point guard at heart.

The Trail Blazers haven't given Portland much to be proud of. It is a dysfunctional team, full of head cases and temperamental malcontents. But in one impromptu moment, Maurice Cheeks gave everyone a reason to be proud.

It has become a touchstone, this act of compassion. There isn't a TV network that hasn't played snippets of the coach coaching the little girl singing the anthem.

There is a reason so many want to show it, to write of it, to celebrate it. Because it resonates so, because it strums one of our most emotional chords, because it reminds us of the stirring capabilities of the human spirit.

"I guess," Maurice Cheeks said, a bit uncomfortable at the thought, "it has become a moment."

Oh, yes. Yes, it has.

One shining moment.

Of grace.

Barkley and the Dream Team: Charles the Diplomat

JULY 26, 1992

The rest of them, the 11 others, double-dribbled all over themselves, desperately trying to be dutiful diplomats. They were inoffensive. They were nonconfrontational. They all but suffered strains and pulls from bending over backward to avoid insulting the world. And they were, frankly, boring.

And then there was the Twelfth Man.

Charles Barkley.

Ever the soul of tact. As always, shrinking from the controversial.

Charles played Spain yesterday, parading his opinions before an overflow, thoroughly enchanted audience. He was, of course, a smash. But then, remember, this is the country that cheers the charging bull. Let us just say that after Barkley's performance, the State Department will not soon be calling to recruit him.

"I love coaching Charles," Chuck Daly sighed. "But I'm glad it's only for these few weeks."

What the others on the Dream Team wouldn't dare say yesterday at a mass media feeding, Barkley would.

And did.

Sometimes without even being asked.

The others mumbled platitudes in defense of the United States' sending an armada of professional players to these "Games of Greed." But when it was his turn, Barkley said: "All those years others sent professional teams. Why is it such a big deal now? Why don't they just take their ass-whipping and go home?"

Michael Jordan hid his head in his hands and slid down in his seat, laughter jiggling his entire body.

The others hedged about Angola, the luckless, opening-round opponent tonight. But Barkley said: "I don't know anything about Angola, but Angola's in trouble."

Larry Bird covered his mouth, but he was too late. You could see the huge grin splitting his face.

The others insisted that, no, there would be no memory of that 1972 robbery/loss to the Soviet Union goading them on. Really, none at all. But

Barkley said: "I had just flunked the entrance exam to kindergarten in '72, but I remember. Yes, there will be a little revenge in our hearts."

Patrick Ewing shook his head, one of those I-can't-believe-the-things-he-says waggles of disbelief.

Magic Johnson, with a straight face, claimed that he bore no ill will toward Australia, whose captain is on record as saying that anyone who is HIV-positive shouldn't be playing in the Olympics. But Barkley volunteered, drawing out each word for emphasis: "Personally, I hope and pray we get to play them. I really do."

Magic Johnson winced and began to slide down to Jordan's level. No use. Neither could disappear.

And so it went yesterday. Barkley, obviously bored, writing checks with his mouth that the Dream Team will have to make good on the court.

Luckily for him, this will not be difficult.

Or, as Barkley replied when asked what opponent might furnish the Dream Team with some semblance of competition: "Croatia, Lithuania, Germany, Spain . . . they could give us a good game."

Pause.

"For a half."

Daly rolled his eyes. He was asked if he had tried to muzzle Barkley, whether he had perhaps suggested to Barkley that he, just for these Olympics, put on a silencer.

"Nope," Daly said pleasantly. "Wouldn't do any good."

And he's right.

Barkley will be Barkley no matter what, no matter if he is in Philadelphia or Phoenix, Monaco or Spain. He will exaggerate and he will overstate and he will infuriate and he will captivate, and always there will be elements of truth in what he says, which is why what he says tends to get people's attention.

He may not always be right, but there will be enough kernels of right in what he says to disturb you. He can be an irritant, but he also can make you think. And that alone makes him worth putting up with.

With the notable exception of Barkley, the Dream Team looked tired and bored. It needs a blood-letting. Barkley is right; Angola is in trouble.

The Dream Team enjoys privileged status. It is exempt from virtually all the usual rules, and this has led to some backbiting and carping by other U.S. athletes.

The main source of disgruntlement is lodging. The Dream Team has a new hotel all to itself while most of the other competitors have to stay in the Village, which is not exactly a tar-paper shack but doesn't have hot and cold running room service, either. Barkley, as usual, cut to the chase:

"It's a little unfair to expect us to stay in the Village when you consider the mystique of Magic and Michael and Larry. We got God on our team and we should stay where God wants us to stay. Right, Michael?"

Jordan was helpless with laughter.

The fact is, this is a special situation. There has never been another contingent like this assembled for an Olympics. That something might happen to it would be a Lloyd's of London worst nightmare.

"It's like traveling with 12 rock stars," Daly said.

It is no exaggeration.

On their only fly-by of the Olympic Village the players were, in Daly's words, "stampeded." They had to be given sanctuary on a bus—and these were other athletes, world-class athletes, who were mobbing them.

The fact is, the Dream Team needs protection.

Normally, it would have come to the right place. An Olympics teems with security. You are X-rayed, tag-checked and otherwise scrutinized at every turn.

And yet as the Dream Team was leaving the stage yesterday, hands eagerly reached out to them, pawing, clutching, hoping for a shake but willing to settle for just a touch.

The hands belonged to uniformed security guards. Only one player managed to shake every one of them.

Bullfights and Basketball: Baskets and Bulls

JULY 27, 1992

On the unforgiving hardwood of the Palace of Sport, amid a lightning storm of flashbulbs, the Dream Team is butchering Angola.

And on the hot sand of the Plaza de Toros Monumental, under an unrelenting summer sun, the matadors are butchering the bulls.

Death in the afternoon.

In both places.

In one arena, on the first day of competition in the Summer Olympics, a hopelessly overmatched basketball team is being bludgeoned by the best sneakered mercenaries money can buy. At least it is harmless entertainment.

In the other arena, great beasts are being put to death, slowly, often clumsily, and you leave feeling ashamed.

Hemingway lied. There is nothing romantic at all about bullfighting, not if you care about animals. It is the systematic mutilation of fearsome but essentially helpless beasts. Torture dressed up in a gold suit.

You came into the first day of competition in these "Games of Greed," thinking that maybe the bulls had a better chance than Angola.

You were wrong.

The losers at the Palace of Sport posed happily afterward, with their conquerors, for keepsake photos. The ravaged corpses of the losers at the Plaza de Toros Monumental were chained by their horns to a team of three Clydesdales and dragged away.

At least the Angolans, opening-round sacrifices to the American armada, the most extravagantly talented team ever drafted for overkill, can fondly reminisce about their day in the sun.

They can gather their children and recall how they had been privileged to be swooped upon by the birdman Jordan and to be mesmerized by the magician Johnson and to be trampled by the rhino Barkley.

And they will recall how the score was once 7-7. Really. And, oh, how plucky they were, how unafraid. And then a great hush will fall as they tell how the American gods called down great clouds of baskets upon them, and how the score swelled and swelled until what had been 7-7 had become 53-8.

The American gods had brought down a cloudburst of 46-1 on them, and they would not even have had that one lonesome point had not the rhino Barkley tried to drive his elbow through the breastbone of the unsuspecting Herlander Coimbra, who was wearing the red number eight, and that earned for the rhino Barkley a technical foul.

And the children's eyes will grow wider and rounder, for of such deeds are legends woven and great memories made.

There are only nightmares made at Plaza de Toros Monumental.

The arena in which the bulls were degraded yesterday seats 20,000. It was not half full, and many of those who had come seemed to be tourists. After all, have we not been told that this is the sport of the daring and the valorous?

The first bull, black and large, a freight train with horns, comes galloping into the circle of hot sand, head swiveling.

They are bred and reared to be perpetually mad, and this one is a snorting engine of destruction. The tormentors encircle him. They call to him, taunting. They flick their scarlet capes, which send him into raging anger. They run him in endless circles, and just as he seems to catch them, they scamper behind thick planking, and he gouges at it in frustration.

They run him and tease him and goad him, working in relays, until his short, stubby legs wobble with fatigue, until his breath is gone, until he stands in one place, glaring at them.

And then come the picadors—two men, armored, astride horses swathed in heavy padding. The horses are kept blindfolded, else they would resist. They would balk, dig their hooves into the sand and refuse to go on, for they know what the horns can do.

Indeed, yesterday one of the bulls caught a horn under the padding. The horse whinnied in terror while the bull wrestled it to the sand, over on its side. The bull yanked its head upward in spasms of instinct, the horn goring only the padding, while the horse thrashed about on the hot sand, unable to rise.

It took eight men, hot and cursing and desperate, to finally separate the bull and horse.

The picadors each carry a long, steel-tipped lance, and as the bull comes at the horse, its head lowered, they drive the lance into its huge back, just behind the massive shoulders, and then they twist and gouge, and when the lance comes out, blood comes out with each heartbeat of the bull, and then it runs down the bull's forelegs and soaks into the hot sand.

And then come the banderilleros—three men, on foot, nimble and quick, each carrying two shorter lances.

They flit around the bull, darting in and plunging the lances into the back, into the same spot behind the shoulders, where the blood comes from the picadors' punctures, and then they dash away, and the bull turns in rage and pain, but he cannot catch his tormentors.

And they come again with the scarlet capes and they turn the bull in circles of frustration, and he becomes dizzy and he slows, and pretty soon he does not turn at all.

And then comes the matador, with his sword hidden in the cape, and he coaxes one more slow charge from the bull, and then one more, and each one is slower, and then the bull's head comes down and the spot just behind the horns, on the back, the spot of death, is bared.

The bull, wounded fatally, his blood running down his back and down his legs and into the hot sand of Plaza de Toros Monumental, stands and looks at the matador and waits to be killed.

And the matador goes up on his toes. Once. Twice. And he sights along his sword, and then he lunges, driving the sword deep into the bull, and then he leaps aside.

But this matador is inept. He botches the killing.

The first sword thrust brings more blood, but not death. The second thrust goes so deep that the sword will not come out and the matador must let go of the handle and leap away. The bull makes one violent shudder of that magnificent back, and the sword comes out and lands in the hot sand.

The matador is whistled off in disgrace and dishonor.

The bull sinks to its knees.

An executioner comes out and stabs the great beast with a knife, just behind the horns. He stabs once. Then again.

The bull bellows, rolls over on its side, but tries to rise.

The executioner stabs the bull again. And again. And again. And yet again.

At last, the stubby legs stiffen. The band plays. The Clydesdales come out, and what is left of a defiled creature is dragged off the hot sand of the Plaza de Toros Monumental.

Another bull will be coming out soon.

Later, those who have stayed come back and tell you that the other matadors were better. They were not as clumsy.

But what does it matter?

Murder is still murder.

John Chaney:
A Fisher of Souls

NOVEMBER 1998

The morning has the feel of a morgue. Everything is Gothic gray. Someone says that it's dawn, but it can't be dawn because the sun isn't up yet. But the Old Man is up. Oh my yes, you bet he's up, waiting for them, watching them through those dark–hollowed raccoon eyes as they come stumbling through the door in their baggy sweats, rubbing the sleep from their eyes, reaching for a donut, taking a bite they don't really taste.

The clock may say that it's only a quarter to sunrise, but here at Temple University they go by Old Man Time. John Chaney Time. Time for learnin'. A little about basketball and a whole lot about life.

He wants first crack at them, wants to be the first voice inside their heads each day, wants to be the first chalk mark on their mental blackboards. And then when he sends them away, he knows that after they have gone to class and put in a full day, they will be too tired for mischief…and if they're not, if they're tempted, all they have to remember is that quarter to sunrise will come very, very early.

No matter how ungodly the hour the Owls practice, there is almost always an audience. Visitors abound. Coaches, mostly, and assistants. Some of them come a long, long way, as though on a pilgrimage. They all have the same answer for their presence: "My boss thought it'd be a good idea. Said I'd be sure to learn something, pick up something."

Billy King, who played against one of John Chaney's very best teams when he was at Duke, is now the personnel man for the Philadelphia 76ers and is a regular at Temple practices. Because? "Because it's like attending the Church of Basketball."

Well, the man in charge can sound like a Pentecostal preacher, rouse you to action, inflame you with evangelical righteousness. Then in the next breath he can scald your posterior with salty profanity. And then turn right around and invoke the soaring grandeur of the poet. All in that distinctive, hoarse rasp. In the off–season, John Chaney's voice never sounds any better than that of a man who has been clinging to a piece of driftwood in the middle of the ocean, screaming for help for three days. By the time the season begins, he is reduced to a whispered shout.

But they never fail to hear him. They hear him a continent away. They hear him from a distance of 10 years, 20, 30. And when they can't hear him with their memory, then they call him so they can hear him again. They put up with his yelling and driving and scolding them, and they dream of the day when they no longer will have to listen to that voice. And then when they are delivered, when they are finally free of it, they discover—irony of ironies—that they miss it so that they ache to hear it again, to hear the familiar parables, the stories with morals.

It is a rare, rare day when the cramped little office of John Chaney does not have an ex–player who has dropped by, or when his phone is not ringing, one more ex–player calling to bust on him, to catch up, to reminisce, to hear one more parable.

Five of them, all in the NBA now, five who could afford it, chipped in to buy him his own suite, number 107, when the Apollo, Temple's new pleasure palace, opened for business. It was a healthy, six–figure purchase.

You ask him about that, about their steadfast loyalty, and he cannot speak. His voice goes thick and husky. Funny thing about the Old Man; he can be off choking an opposing coach one moment, raging and frighteningly out of control, and then the next someone is asking about one of his kids and he is crying like an Irishman overcome by a particularly entrancing sunset.

The one night of the year John Chaney dreads is Senior Night. Two or three of his fledglings play their last home game and he is always a blubbering mess. He hugs them roughly and they end up being the ones who have to console him. "Here, coach, use my handkerchief."

Frequently, they will spend more of those predawns sitting on the hardwood floor and listening to sermonettes and colorful, street–corner versions of Aesop's Fables than they will with an actual basketball in their hands.

In the words of Speedy Morris, the La Salle coach: "A message about life every day. How many coaches give their kids that?"

Even though he went past 600 wins last season, a total achieved by only a couple of handfuls of coaches, there are a lot of people in Philadelphia who believe that just about the least important thing John Chaney does is coach basketball. One of those people happens to be the Old Man's boss. Temple president Peter Liacouras has this to say: "John is in the business of giving people a chance. That's supposed to be part of the mission of education, isn't it? He's a perfect fit here. He is always saying that when you refuse a kid a chance, it's like the Statue of Liberty turning her back on the huddled masses."

The Old Man reaches out to the impoverished and the disadvantaged, and he rails against exclusivity, against tests and standards of measurement that he sees as designed to keep kids out rather than let them in. Temple routinely takes kids that others refuse. In many ways, he is a fisher of souls. His ratio of salvation to failure is high. Doesn't matter—he mourns over every one that gets away, the ones he hasn't been able to reach, even though he pretends good riddance. In the end, what matters is not who came in the back door but what, four or five years later, you are sending out the front door.

The Old Man has no use for pretense and airs. He and his wife have lived in the same three–bedroom rowhouse for going on half a century. They raised three kids there. "What do we need more room for now?" he yelps. He has few extravagances, but expensive ties are among them. Invariably, though, the tie is at limp half–mast by game's start, and the coach looks like his clothier is Rumpled & Wrinkled, Inc. If the Owls lose, the bad–luck necktie is given away to the first taker.

The coach will begin the game calmly enough, and on occasion will lean back and cover his face with his hands, as though he has not the slightest interest in what is transpiring on the court, or cannot bear to look. It is all an elaborate pose, of course. When the time is running out, and if the game is close, one that has become stealable, then he lowers himself on one arthritic knee, leans an elbow on the scorers' table, and begins to fuss at them.

There is absolutely nothing joyous at all about playing Temple. It is a drudge—painful and aesthetically inelegant and frustrating, especially if what you want to do with the ball is run, run, run. The pace is grinding. Each possession becomes magnified in importance because there won't be as many possessions as there customarily are in a game. Temple will play that confounding match–up zone and the Owls will hardly ever turn the ball over, mainly because the Old Man has them believing that committing turnovers will get you roasted in hell. If you are making a good percentage of your long–range jumpshots, then you have a chance. If you are not, you are going to be embarrassed, and it will be only scant consolation that over the years you have had loads of company.

If there is a call that goes against Temple that is perceived by the Old Man to be especially egregious, then he will set off into a foaming rant. He may fix the offending zebra with a withering glare that he describes as his "one–eyed Jacks stare." Or he may totally lose it and try to charge out onto the floor, and one of his assistants, and sometimes even his players, will have to physically restrain him. These are invariably embarrassing moments, seeing a man close to 70 unable to exercise self–control, seeing such an extraordinary teacher and such a remarkable mentor reduced to thuggish ways.

His defense is that he will be the noisemaker, and he alone. If someone is to be embarrassed, let it fall on him. In his own words, "I can be an ass at times, but I don't want my kids to be one." And yes, there is some hypocrisy inherent in that—do as I preach to you, but most assuredly not as I occasionally lapse into doing.

Here is a coach who adamantly prohibits taunting or trash–talking. His players are strictly forbidden to trade high–fives, or to belly–bump or punch the air. There will be no showing up the opponent and no unseemly displays of self–celebration. Respect the opponent, respect the game. The penalty for violation is benching, swiftly imposed and for an indeterminate time.

"I won't permit them to give in to emotion, because you can get drunk on emotion," he says.

Yet he himself is routinely so intoxicated.

But balanced against his impressive body of work, judged in the context of lives saved and altered and forever impacted, it is excused as pardonable, a tolerable flaw.

And rage—after all, passion—is what has fueled him all his life. He's spent so much time fighting for everything that it is what he reverts to even now, that instinct, in moments of distress.

Chaney was a guard himself. He took care of the ball as though it were a vital body part. He was the Public League player of the year in Philadelphia his senior year. He had to borrow a hand–me–down suit to go to the banquet. It hung on him shapelessly, and he hid in the restroom in shame and wept. When he went away to college, to Bethune–Cookman in Florida, all of his belongings fit into a cardboard box that he carried under his arm. He became a small–college All–American and graduated in 1955 with a degree in health and physical education. He coached for 15 years in Philadelphia public schools and then for 10 years at Cheyney State, where he won a Division II national championship.

Peter Liacouras hired Chaney in 1982. The Old Man was already 50. "Didn't matter," Liacouras said. "Sometimes, younger isn't better." He was right.

The years had weathered Chaney. The Owls began to win, almost from his first day, and they haven't stopped. He has been named national coach of the year twice. It is a given that Temple will be in the NCAA tournament virtually every year, and also a given that the Owls are one team everyone else dreads drawing.

The combative part of John Chaney, the part that relishes being the underdog, is the one insisting on the murderous schedule. The Owls will play anyone, anywhere, any time. By March, they are cold steel. They don't care where the brackets send them. Publicly, the Old Man will moan when the Owls get exiled 3,000 miles away, to someplace in Idaho, say. But secretly, he will exult because he knows his players have been prepared, that the rigors of such a trip will not faze them because they have spent all year playing in hostile, faraway places.

Temple can be a hard sell to a potential recruit. It is largely a commuter campus. It isn't Chapel Hill. Or Brentwood. Or Tempe. And there are those quarter–to–dawn practices with the Old Man yelling at you and then sitting you down and lecturing you about life. Who needs that?

Well, as we know by now, quite a few people.

11

Goodbyes . . .
to Absent Friends

Tug McGraw:
True Believer

JANUARY 6, 2004

The cancer may have left him bloated and bald, but not beaten. Oh, no, not beaten. Surrender was unthinkable. He would never give in. Never.

If you spend a large chunk of your life pitching the bottom of the ninth, then the thought of ever relenting is beyond your imagining. And so he was defiant to the very end.

He was the candle that burned on.

Frank Edwin McGraw, Irish leprechaun and blithe spirit, was a man who claimed to be able to speak the language of the dolphins and made you believe it. Even with that insidious disease's death sentence hanging over him, he remained full of joy, still wringing the juices from life, still spreading the gospel of hope and resistance and persistence. He looked a terrible killer full in the eye, laughed in its face, then offered to buy it a round. His courage and the fierceness of his spirit made you weep.

Early last evening, Tug McGraw breathed his last. It is a loss that leaves us all diminished. And yet in the midst of sorrow survives his legacy, the lust for life, the friends made, the toasts made and drunk, the laughter that rattled the roof, the stories spun, the memories rekindled, the dawns greeted, the sunsets saluted.

He was left–handed in all of the best ways. His best pitch was a screw-ball—and how altogether fitting that was.

"They only call you a 'screwball' till you make a pile of money," Tug would say, "and then they start calling you 'eccentric.'"

The scroogie is hard on the elbow, requiring a violent, wrenching spasm, but his was even harder on the hitters, who would flail impotently at it and were left muttering to themselves as they slunk back to the dugout, unused bats trailing behind them. They might as well have tried to hit a Frisbee in a high wind.

And he would, at inning's end, make that duck-footed, bouncy, up-on-the-balls-of-the-feet walk from the mound, slapping his glove against his chest in an exaggerated show of relief and release.

Tug was a showman without being a showoff. He loved the game and never shrank from showing that passion. He would wrap the moment in an unabashed bear hug, thankful for the chance just to be playing—and, my, how you wish the new breed of today would follow his example instead of wearing those perpetual scowls.

In mid-March, they found two tumors in his brain. After the surgery, the medical report was: "He is in good spirits." And you thought: Well, of course he is. When isn't he?

It's hard to know exactly how many candles were lit for him, how many prayers offered up in the cool darkness of a sanctuary. But the outpouring of affection was immense.

Tug hadn't thrown a ball in the bigs in a generation, yet he was beloved in Philadelphia. There are a very few freeze-frames of sports moments in this city's history that will last, and one of the most luminous is that October night in 1980, Game 6 of the World Series, Tug McGraw sneaking his Peggy Lee fastball ("Is that all there is?") past Willie Wilson. And then he danced an Irish jig on the mound, arms aimed at the heavens, waiting for Mike Schmidt to leap upon him, followed by an avalanche of Phillies teammates.

That was just yesterday, wasn't it? What? Was it 23 years ago? No, it couldn't be. Could it?

"You're getting old, my friend," he said. And then he laughed and added: "Me, too. But at least we still have the memory."

Tug was here often, last summer and in the autumn. All manner of organizations and charities wanted to honor him, wanted to hear him speak of cancer, and he would oblige, gracious and funny, his spirit unflagging.

Relief pitchers tend to be, well, the polite word is different.

"What you mean," he said, "is on the far side of . . . well, out there beyond where it gets weird."

The more you watched him, the more you thought you'd like to visit out there beyond.

A lot of games were entrusted to the care of Tug McGraw. He preserved most of them. And he had a roaring great time doing it.

"Ya Gotta Believe" was his slogan. He invented it while he was with the Mets, but it stuck to him like Velcro when he was with the Phillies, and afterward, right up to the end.

It will forever remain his motto, but he wouldn't mind a bit if you'd like to adopt it for yourself.

Bear Bryant:
Alabama Mourning

JANUARY 28, 1983

A shroud covers Alabama. The sky leaks, and it is murky and almost Gothic, and the winter drizzle is persistent.

"It started raining early Wednesday afternoon," said Denise Morgan at the airport car-rental counter. She paused and thought, and then added: "You know, it started raining just about the time he died."

She said it like it was symbolic. Maybe it was.

A whole state is in mourning. Bear Bryant is dead, and a deep melancholy has settled in.

This is the way it must have felt in the South when Lee handed over his sword to Grant at Appomattox. For Bear Bryant was a towering legend down here—a genuine folk hero, regarded with a reverence Southerners reserve for a Robert E. Lee, a Stonewall Jackson.

"What can I say?" asked Melford Espeedy, director of campus activities at the University of Alabama. "I equate him with Patton, Churchill and Roosevelt."

Added Thomas A. Bartlett, chancellor of the university: "It's the untimely end of an authentic hero. We have too few heroes in our society. To see one passing is a great loss."

That probably hits on it.

For Bear Bryant was perceived as more than just a football coach. He was Alabama's savior. To a state that is not held in particularly high esteem by outsiders, who regard it as one of the last bastions of poverty, prejudice and pettiness, Bear Bryant was their rallying point, their lodestone of pride. Everyone respected the Bear, and in the minds of the people this was atonement for them; his success was their success. When Alabama won, they all won.

It is why followers of the Crimson Tide treated each Saturday afternoon in the autumn as a crusade, why each national championship the Bear's boys secured was so celebrated, so cherished. Alabama might not be number one in anything else, but by damn it had the best darn helmet-bustin', hell-for-leather, gang-tacklin' football team in the country.

Bryant sensed this himself, and so it was that he toasted each triumph as victory for the mamas and daddies of those little ol' pine knots who had played their hearts out and brought recognition to Alabama.

"Rollllllllll Tide" became an impassioned shout of defiance, a sort of modern Rebel yell.

Governor George Wallace sensed this, too. Long ago, he had officially conferred upon Bryant the label of "one of our state's greatest natural resources," and anointed him Alabama's number one asset.

Wallace personally announced the passing of Bryant to the state Senate and immediately ordered all flags to half-staff. And the governor appeared on television yesterday, eyes red-rimmed, and said: "No one can ever replace him. He brought so much fame and credit to our state. There will never be another like him."

That is why the melancholy is so thick here. The South has lost a symbol. The tallest of the Dixie pines is gone.

In its lead editorial yesterday, the *Birmingham News* touched on this: "The gridiron achievements of Bryant the coach—though certainly awesome—were not nearly so important to Alabama's psyche as was Bryant the symbol. He was the epitome of the Southern spirit, a dirt-poor farm boy who through his own talent, determination and strength of character rose up from poverty to inspire the respect of an entire nation.

"He was excellence personified under the halo of a houndstooth hat. He was toughness, tempered by a rare kindness, and the gruff but ever-humble expressions of a man who never forgot his roots or his friends. . . . But most of all, he was ours. He will live on in the minds of millions, standing beside a goal post, hat cocked, eyes squinting down a football field . . . and with the heart of Alabama at his side."

The entire front page of yesterday's edition was devoted to Bryant— four stories, plus a color drawing, and an epitaph in the form of this quote from New Orleans Saints coach Bum Phillips when he was a Bryant assistant: "Coach Bryant doesn't coach football. He coaches people."

Birmingham has been called the Pittsburgh of the South, a steel city down amidst the magnolia and the pine. But hard times have visited here and overstayed their welcome. Unemployment is at a raging high and most of the blast furnaces and open hearths stand still and cold. The steel industry is facing third-and-long and no one seems to have a trick play for the occasion.

There was temporary relief each Saturday when the Bear would lead out his team and whomp somebody good. It helped make the bitterness go down a little easier. But then, a month ago, he coached his last game, and now, so suddenly, he is gone. And with him went Alabama's principal source of comfort, its chestiest pride.

Listen to the mourners:

Shirley Oswalt, sales clerk in Tuscaloosa: "He's kind of been the spirit of Alabama for so long."

Mike McCrory, Birmingham ticket agent: "I was really sad to hear about it because he was one of the positive things going for the state. He sure was. He was one of the best."

Mrs. Haynie Smith, Tuscaloosa teacher: "It's like you've lost a member of the family. He's in everyone's home."

That is why the grieving is felt so deeply, why the sobs of mourning are so wrenching and the mourners are so inconsolable. Nothing is forever, but it seemed to the people of Alabama that if anything could be, it would be Bear Bryant.

Terri Price, a 26-year-old sales clerk at the Parisian department store in Birmingham, said simply: "There was just always Bear. Just like there was always Jesus."

No one protested that this smacked of blasphemy, for here Bear Bryant was as close to being a deity as a mortal can get. Alabama wears its grief on its sleeve today.

The papers are filled with in memoriam ads and the marquees of motels carry neon messages like, "We'll Miss You, Bear" and "Thanks for the Memories."

TV stations, newspapers and the phone company all reported that telephone traffic minutes after the bulletin of Bryant's death was the highest since President Reagan had been shot nearly two years ago. At the Eastwood Mall in Birmingham, the Bear Bryant Souvenir Shop was selling out its supply of T-shirts, ashtrays, busts and other Bryant memorabilia.

"This was just a general souvenir shop in the beginning," said Richard Williams, the manager, "but Bear was so popular that's all anyone wanted, mementos of him. So a few years ago, we just specialized in him." Yesterday, customers came and bought in hushed whispers, as though they were at a shrine.

WBRC-TV in Birmingham broadcast file film on its noon report yesterday, rare locker room footage of a younger Bryant addressing an Alabama team that was behind at halftime. "Keep your heads up," he was saying in a low, gutteral voice, "and if you've got class, it'll all work out."

At the conclusion of the film, the news anchor said: "I don't know what else can be said." And he lowered his head to hide his tears.

A radio sports-talk show host had opened his lines to "whoever wants to talk about the Bear" on Wednesday night. He stayed on the air for seven straight hours and the switchboard was still lit.

But Bryant will not lie in state. There will be no public viewing of the body.

A memorial service was held on the Tuscaloosa campus late yesterday afternoon, and the public was urged to attend that rather than the funeral in Tuscaloosa and burial in Birmingham, 58 miles away, today.

Thus, the marking of his passage will be swift. Barely 48 hours will have elapsed from the time Bear Bryant died to the time of his interment. It is as though its grief is so crushing that Alabama cannot stand the thought of prolonging its goodbyes.

Given the depth of their loss, that is understandable.

Mickey Mantle:
A Life Reclaimed

AUGUST 14, 1995

He died by inches and he died mostly by his own hand, and he died while all of us were watching. But there is a shining triumph, too, in Mickey Mantle's passing. For of all the mythical things he did as a baseball player, his most inspiring moments came toward the end.

For of all the glory he may have achieved on the playing field, his most ennobling acts occurred on his deathbed. Mickey Mantle died with dignity, having made his peace, which is all any of us can hope for, and in the doing of that demonstrated how it is possible, and never too late, to repent and, more important, to reform.

For years our memories of him have been of this enormously talented switch-hitter belting mighty home runs. But the image that lingers now, the one that will remain with us, is not of the robust athlete with that odd mixture of shyness and arrogance, nor of the churlish card-show drunk hiking his trousers so that icon-worshiping tycoons could ogle the surgical scars on his knees.

No, the image that will last is of a frail, wasted man with a shrunken face, unsparing and unsympathetic to himself, somehow summoning the courage to stand up in public, grin that engaging, lopsided grin, and say: "I'm a role model. Right here. Look. I'm a model for what not to do. Don't be like me."

The other day I heard a man—a doctor yet—say that Mickey Mantle had stolen a liver.

That was the exact word he used. Stolen.

The man argued that the organ should have been transplanted into someone else, into someone who was more worthy, more deserving; into someone who was not quite as far gone as Mantle was; into someone whose body was not already hopelessly eaten by cancer; into someone whose survival might be measured in years rather than in days and so might make better use of it.

And I thought: What a cruel and heartless thing to say.

In the passing of his cold judgment, the man was implying that the doctors treating Mantle knew him to be terminal, even before performing the liver transplant, and in doing so, "wasted" a perfectly good organ.

But Mickey Mantle eloquently rebutted this unfeeling slander by the way he lived out his last days. In the two months between his transplant and his death, he wrung from that new liver a lifetime's worth of good deeds and redemptive acts. A wasted transplant? I think not. Who knows how many lives Mickey Mantle may have altered at the end, how many souls he may have salvaged?

No single person in memory has served as such a compelling example of the devastation that alcohol abuse can bring as Mickey Mantle did every time he spoke so movingly of the waste he had caused, every time his dying face appeared on our TV screens. Alcoholics must have thought they were seeing Marley's ghost.

For all the harm and hurt he caused others in most of his 63 years, Mickey Mantle tried to undo the damage and to atone in his last year and a half, starting with the publication of his autobiography and his public confession of his destructive drinking.

The mostly positive reception he got startled him. But then he never had understood the hold he had. His popularity astonished him, particularly as it grew after he retired. He is one of the few players who became more esteemed after he had left the game than when he was playing it. But when he realized he was dying, he seemed also to grasp, at last, the sway he held, the influence he could have, and he channeled it in the best direction he could.

There can be nothing quite so pathetic, quite so sad, as a drunk. Ironically, there can also be nothing quite so heroic, quite so reaffirming, as a recovering drunk.

Mickey Mantle's life was a Faustian bargain. He was granted great talent, but the price was the torment and the ruin of the self-destructive.

It became popular to portray him as another familiar American tragedy, an artist of sorts blessed with singular skills who squanders those gifts. Yet it is not the artistry, the performances, we will recall so much, nor the celebrated debauchery, but rather the way he approached the end and what he was able to reclaim from it.

Howard Porter:
A Man Redeemed

JUNE 5, 2007

His special genius was fashioned out of scavenged junk. The backboard was a cracked plank of plywood, the basket was a rusted bicycle tire rim, and the ball, thrown out with someone else's garbage, had been dribbled until the seams were worn smooth. And by the light of the Florida sun and of the silvery moon, night and day, day and night, the sweat running off him in little rivers, he honed his jump shot to silky perfection.

He would grow to six feet eight, with cannonball shoulders, and he moved with a feline grace, cheetah-sleek. His childhood was one of grinding hopelessness, of fatherless impoverishment, his future a certain dead end. The only way out was through the Oscar Robertson instructional basketball booklet his mother bought, and then a million jump shots followed by 10 million more.

Howard Porter scuffled his way out of despair and that certain dead end, all the way to the Main Line. From 1967 through 1971, he played 89 games for Villanova, scored 2,006 points, grabbed 1,317 rebounds and blocked shots with such looming fury that cowed opponents became gun-shy. His game was equal parts suppleness and strength, and he made all-America three straight seasons. The man known as "Geezer," likable and cordial, also made hundreds of friends.

In the middle of his senior season, he succumbed to temptation. An agent offered him a signing bonus of $15,000 to put his name on an ABA contract, that league then in competition with the NBA and desperate for talent. If you've never had 15 dollars in your whole life, what must 15 thousand look like?

Porter drove 'Nova all the way to the Final Four in 1971 and into the championship game against John Wooden's UCLA dynasty. 'Nova lost, barely, and Porter was named the most outstanding player. The balloting wasn't even close. His transgression was soon discovered, his name replaced in the record books by vacated—a cold and unforgiving word. And in those same record books, national runner-up Villanova was labeled with an asterisk that has remained as permanent as a tattoo. From a distance of 36 years, and in the context of all that goes on today, his transgression seems almost benign. But not then. Then, forgiveness was not immediately forthcoming.

Howard Porter's anguish was bone-deep. It would last a long, bitter time, and it would, ultimately, drive him to ruin. Shamed, he distanced himself from his school. His pro career lasted seven mostly undistinguished seasons, truncated by injury. His marriage splintered. He turned for solace to white powder, the stuff of enchanted dreams and wretched reality. He became a cocaine addict and a drifter, pawning his Final Four watch and any other trinkets that would buy the next fix and that short-lived, make-the-world-go-away escape. Arrest and imprisonment seemed inevitable, and soon enough became fact.

In one of those quotes that raise the hairs on the nape of your neck, in an interview with the *Minneapolis Star Tribune,* he described his descent into devastation this way: "I took a ride with the devil. And the devil picked me up and rolled me for a while. But I always knew, deep down inside, I felt God wasn't through with me yet."

He was right. He went into rehab in Minnesota and emerged in 1989, clean and sober. He was redemption waiting to happen, a determined example of the fierce, indomitable, unbending human spirit. His first step was to throw off that crushing weight of recrimination that had haunted him for so long.

In a 1996 interview with *Sports Illustrated,* Howard Porter said: "I waited all those years for someone to forgive me, but no one ever did. Finally, I decided just to forgive myself."

His metamorphosis was striking, awe-inspiring. He went back to school and earned his degree from Villanova, in English and psychology. Besides the degree, he earned forgiveness. All those broken fences were mended. In 1997, his number 54 was retired and raised to the Pavilion rafters.

Porter found an angel named Theresa Neal. He became a parole and probation officer in Minnesota, and what sweet irony that was—the man who had made so many mistakes, now trying to keep others from all those same misjudgments, trying to get them to save themselves from themselves.

He became mentor, counselor, confessor—a source of hope and inspiration for the troubled and the tormented.

The sinner had turned into savior. Is there a greater victory?

And then, suddenly, violently, he was gone—found savagely beaten in an alley, then dead eight days later.

It made no sense. A 33-year-old St. Paul woman was arrested Sunday night, according to St. Paul police. But no answers are yet forthcoming. Nor maybe ever will be. Such a bizarre end to such an inspiring story.

His impact was so far-reaching that memorial services are being held in three states: Minnesota, Pennsylvania and Florida. Visitation is this afternoon from five to seven at St. Thomas of Villanova Church, with a memorial liturgy to follow.

Howard Porter crammed a dozen lifetimes into his 58 years, from soaring heights to crushing depths, and back again. He leaves a legacy of a man most mortal, flawed but redeemed, a man who succumbed and toppled, and then arose in glorious triumph.

His spirit burned as fierce as a flame.

A Tie to Celebrate

JANUARY 2002

Before he went straight, Ernie Accorsi made his way by beating words out of a keyboard. He wrote for this newspaper back in the dark ages of typewriters. (Children, ask your parents about those quaint contraptions. Wait, better yet, ask your grandparents.) Eventually he made his way to Baltimore, and one fine day looked around to find himself general manager of a professional football team. The Colts. First as reporter, then as GM, Accorsi could not help but frequently wind up in the company of John Steadman, a courtly man who loved Baltimore, which returned the favor.

John Steadman wrote a sports column for assorted Baltimore newspapers for about half a century. He was impeccably principled and unwavering in his convictions, champion of all causes just. He was an honorable man and as straight as it is possible to be and still be human. He came to be considered the moral conscience of the village, a frightening assignment indeed.

John was gentle in speech. His eyebrows were impressively bushy and permanently arched, somewhere between surprise and reproof. Frequently, they spoke for him. John doted on all things Baltimore, but especially the Colts. He never missed a game. Literally. Between the Colts, and then their successors, the Ravens, John attended 719 consecutive games. It made him the Cal Ripken of this profession. The last few he had to come to in a wheelchair.

Two years ago, he looked up from his desk and said to a colleague: "I think I've caught a bit of a bad break."

As was his way in things involving him, John didn't want to make a fuss about having cancer.

John was an inveterate gift-giver, and he especially delighted in bestowing ties. Gentlemanly in dress as well as deportment, he was never without one around his own neck. Three years ago, on the day that Ernie Accorsi became the general manager of the football Giants, John drove up from Baltimore and presented Accorsi with a congratulatory tie. "It is a bit on the, uh, garish side, isn't it?"

"Uh-huh," Accorsi said fondly.

It's mostly green or blue, with some red, and a lot of tiny golfers running down it. Accorsi has come to think of it as a talisman, and the tie that tethers him to a dear old friend.

On the first day of this year, at the age of 73, after two years of valorous and gallant resistance, John Steadman succumbed to the cancer. Ernie Accorsi went to the funeral, just days before the Giants' playoff game against the Eagles. He needed an hour to get through the line. The whole town had turned out, none more prominent than the old Colts: Johnny Unitas, Lenny Moore, Art Donovan. It looked as if Canton had set up shop in Baltimore.

In honor of John, Accorsi wore the tie to the NFC championship game. The Giants routed the Minnesota Vikings, 41-0.

The Giants are in the Super Bowl. And so are the Ravens of Baltimore, the first time a team from John Steadman's beloved town has been there in 30 years. So many connections, so many, uh, ties.

The hard-eyed cynic will note that a necktie does not throw a pass or catch one, does not make a tackle or miss one. But those in sports are no different than many of the rest of us. In moments of high anxiety and low spirits, we all cling tightly to superstitions, charms, rituals—whatever will sustain us emotionally and spiritually.

So, of course, Ernie Accorsi will wear his special tie one more time.

"I know where John is," he said, "and I know he'll be watching, but I don't know which way he'll be leaning up there, so I'm playing the percentages."

Accorsi stood in the stands at Raymond James Stadium the other day, dressed all in black as though mourning. The sky was high, the sun bright, the air brisk. What, he was asked, if anything, did you take from your days as chronicler?

"Integrity," he said.

Should we report that he said that with a sneer?

"No, I mean it. I'm proud of it."

He smiled.

"At least it proves I wasn't illiterate."

The integrity he picked up hanging around John Steadman.

"He knew what was right. Even when he was hammering us, I said, 'You know, if John is after us, we're probably wrong.'"

The football knowledge he picked up by hanging out with George Halas and Paul Brown and Vince Lombardi and Wellington Mara.

"I'm so grateful for every minute I was in a room with them," he said. "I listened, I observed, I absorbed. Probably the most basic and important thing I learned was that you need great players at the right positions, so spend your money on the positions that have the most impact on the game."

Did he ever despair of ever reaching a Super Bowl?

"Not really. I never gave up hope. I guess because there are just too many stories. . . . I mean, look at [Dick] Vermeil, he's out of the game for years and then comes back and gets in it and wins it."

There is a tie that links Baltimore and New York, and like the tie that Ernie Accorsi will wear Sunday, it is equal parts lore and tradition and history. Teams from the two cities were the combatants in two of the most famous NFL championship games: the 1958 overtime win by the Colts over the Giants and the 1969 Joe Namath–guaranteed victory by the Jets over the Colts.

Those are the sort of ties John Steadman would have relished in exploring this week—Super Bowl XXXV.

He was one of nine writers to have covered the first 34 Super Bowls.

"Two years ago, when it was in Miami, I had just found out that John had started treatment," Accorsi said, "and as soon as I checked into my hotel, I called John. His wife answered and said, 'Ernie, he's staying in the same hotel you're in.' There was no way he wasn't coming."

We fall silent.

After a bit, Ernie Accorsi clears his throat and says: "All those games he came to in a row, went to every Super Bowl, and now not to be here for this one. I miss him here. . . . I miss him. . . . I keep thinking I'll turn around and he'll be there. . . ."

He looks away and reaches for his sunglasses. They are dark as a coal mine. But it isn't the sun that makes him put them on. You wish you had a pair for yourself.

Leonard Tose:
Flair and Flaw

APRIL 16, 2003

Leonard Tose lived half a dozen lifetimes. He made it almost to 90, and in that span crammed in triumph and tragedy, wealth and ruin, riotously destructive gambling and staggeringly generous deeds of compassion and philanthropy.

He was the Great Gatsby of his time, living high and living well, and yet not walled off from people in all stations of life. He could get along with a cardinal just as comfortably as with a truck driver. He was never the snob.

Of all the figures who have wandered across the sporting landscape of this city in the last three decades, Leonard Tose, who died yesterday at age 88, was one of the most memorable, a man of both imposing strengths and disastrous weaknesses.

He was dashing and debonair. He loved his football team, and yet almost ruined it. He often couldn't help himself but spent most of a lifetime helping others.

What lingers still is the memory of the helicopter he had decked out in the Eagles colors, green and white, and used to taxi him to team practices. This was in the '70s, and the chopper would descend onto the field at Widener University with clamorous noise and fanfare. Out would step the owner, always dapper, producing plumes of smoke from his ever-present cigarette. People couldn't help but gape. Leonard Tose always did have a flair for the grand entrance.

He was a man of modest build but blessed with the constitution of a horse. He smoked like a chimney, drank rivers of scotch, underwent open-heart surgery three decades ago when that procedure was not nearly as successful as it is now, traded in wives like he traded in limos, and yet almost to the end had a robust love of life. There couldn't have been much that he didn't experience.

His final days were spent in a reclusive exile. Irretrievably mired in debt, he had all that he owned sold out from under him, the proceeds divided among his creditors. Once Tose had millions, but at the end he was dependent upon handouts from those he had befriended earlier, when he was flush.

One of his biggest benefactors was Dick Vermeil, whom Tose had hired to coach the Eagles. It was a daring move at the time because Vermeil was a college coach without pro experience, and much to the distaste of Iggles loyalists, he was "one of them West Coast guys," meaning he probably wouldn't be tough enough for Philly. Vermeil, of course, ended up being the only Eagles coach ever to produce a Super Bowl team.

"Leonard was a coach's dream for an owner," Vermeil said once. "He never interfered and all he ever told me was: 'Whatever you need, we'll get for you.'"

Leonard Tose had an appetite for life's pleasures, and in the end he became a victim of that appetite. He went through a sizable fortune at the blackjack tables. He had a penchant for renting an entire table for himself and then playing all seven hands simultaneously—each hand $10,000.

It was not unusual, he said, for him to sign a million dollars' worth of markers in an evening. His gambling ended up costing him his beloved football team. And it very nearly cost Philadelphia its beloved football team. The Philadelphia Eagles were on the brink of becoming the Phoenix Eagles because Leonard Tose couldn't pay off all the gambling IOUs that he had accumulated, by his own testimony, through drunk and sloppy gambling. An automobile dealer named Norman Braman bought the team and kept it in his hometown.

What often has been obscured over the years because of the gambling is all of the charitable work that Leonard Tose did. He was the softest of soft touches. For all his own self-destructive habits, he was quick to open his checkbook for any cause he deemed worthy. He was the financial angel for a lot of people down on their luck and for those in need. The glittering monument that lives on after him is the Eagles Fly for Leukemia drive, and the Ronald McDonald Houses that are found all over the world. Those are works of wondrous generosity.

On occasion he would call, and whether you answered or your machine did, his greeting was always the same: "Yes, it's Leonard Tose calling . . . T-O-S-E."

He spelled it slowly and carefully, as though you might confuse him with anyone else. No chance of that, Leonard. No chance at all.